# Self-Transformation and Second Chances

DICKENS'S TALE OF
HOPE AND REDEMPTION

## Louis A. Marini

PAGE PUBLISHING
Conneaut Lake, PA

First originally published by Page Publishing 2023

ISBN 979-8-88654-642-2 (pbk)
ISBN 979-8-88654-646-0 (digital)

Printed in the United States of America

In memory of my parents, Serafina and Lucio,
who demonstrated faith, warmth, kindness, and
the Christmas spirit every day of the year.
Their self-giving love and devotion to family were their
greatest gifts to us in celebrating the Lord's birth.

# CONTENTS

One would be better served to either read for the first time or reread Dickens's great classic *A Christmas Carol* before engaging in this book. Even if you have viewed the many adaptions of *A Christmas Carol on the screen*, I encourage you to read this wonderful tale. The references in this book will be highlighting scenes of the written version of this masterpiece as it was written by Charles Dickens in 1843. I have provided a brief summary of the tale in the appendix of the book for those who have not had the opportunity to familiarize themselves with this work.

This novella clearly exhibits how faith and self-transformation are redemptive of the human condition. It is noteworthy that upon publishing the first edition of *A Christmas Carol*, Dickens had his sixty-six-page heavily revised handwritten manuscript bound in crimson leather and decorated in gilt before gifting it to his friend and creditor Thomas Mitton, whose name was also inscribed on the cover in gilt.[1]

The first edition of six thousand copies accorded to his colleague and friend John Forster was sold on the day of publication, and about as many more would seem to have been disposed of before the end of February 1844.[2]

The story of *A Christmas Carol* is every person's journey of faith, self-transformation, and redemption. This tale teaches us that it is not only how dear we hold the past and present experiences of our lives but also how we finally end up when death knocks at our door that tells our story. Although both the joys and trials of life make us stronger and resilient, it is in the latter years of our lives that we realize how fortunate we have been to have had the opportunity to meet the people who have changed our lives. This realization sheds light on who we are and how significant we are in the course of what we have learned and accomplished in our lives. It is the maturation of our earthly years that gives us a better perspective in how we have made a difference in our world. It is our relationships with people not necessarily our personal accomplishments that will shine in the long run when our stories are told.

Our lives are like earthen vessels, fragile but unbreakable, due to our self-determination and steadfast faith. Faith allows us the opportunity to make the needed changes so that life is worth the journey. Despite the regrets, failures, and misgivings of our past, we still can change. Faith is the foundation, anchor, and at the root of self-transformation.

Self-transformation is the result of change, which is always possible in the course of our lives, although it becomes more challenging as we age. The process of transformation tells us that to be truly, fully, and authentically human is to be divine; anything less needs forgiveness.

Faith is the foundation of that process. Kelly Clarkson, an American singer and songwriter who in her song "Stronger," suggests that being human carries with it the resiliency that "what doesn't kill you makes you stronger." Human life is unique in the sense that transformation at any age is always possible and never too late or fully achieved until we have breathed our last. Second chances are always possible. In a sense, we live for second chances. My purpose in authoring this book, a sequel to my previous book entitled *The Faith: A Human Reality and a Divine Mystery*, is to highlight Dickens's tale of *A Christmas Carol* as to demonstrate how faith and self-transformation are redemptive of the human condition.

All of us at one time or another have exhibited shortsightedness and self-centeredness as characterized in the life of the infamous fictitious character of Ebenezer Scrooge. We have also experienced the joys that self-giving brings, which Scrooge comes to experience subsequently in reclaiming his life. Life is a mixed bag of varied experiences. Some bring us shame and regret while others bring us pride and joy. Only those of us who exhibit self-giving and compassion are truly the real Dickens heroes. As legendary as *A Christmas Carol* is in the halls of the world's literature being considered the most famous Christmas tale ever written, it transcends the Christmas spirit of joy and cheer. All Dickens's great gifts seem reflected, sharp and distinct, in this little book as in a convex mirror.[3] It is the story of how the ghosts of Christmas past, present, and to come each in turn speaks to the weazened heart of the old miser so that, almost unwittingly, he is softened by the tender memories of childhood, warmed by sympathy for those who struggle and suffer, and appalled by the prospect of his own ultimate desolation and black solitude.[4] In short, it is a story of how faith becomes the foundation of self-transformation and how transformation results in human redemption. It is a tale of second chances.

We can easily relate with many of the colorful characters of *A Christmas Carol.* Whether it is the ambitious and profit-seeking drive of Jacob Marley, the loving-kindness and understanding of a devoted husband and father as Bob Cratchit, or the optimistic personality of Scrooge's nephew Fred, all of us have been there. We can identify with the enthusiasm and playfulness as portrayed by the Cratchit children or the optimism and self-giving persona of Mrs. Cratchit. We can relate to the generosity and collaborative spirit of Mr. Fezziwig and the virtues of perseverance and persistence as seen by the two unnamed gentlemen who solicited funds for the poor and the destitute in the opening pages of the tale. We can identify with Scrooge's sister Fan who characterizes those friends and family members of ours who are relentlessly in our corner in difficult and trying times. We can appreciate the power of love in relationship as expressed by Scrooge's fiancée, Belle. Finally, we are showered with hope and serenity as reflected in the goodness and innocence as personified by Tiny Tim.

All of us in various degrees have been haunted by our own personal ghosts in the past, haunted by our own struggles and demons in the present, and troubled by anxieties and restlessness of future uncertainties. I would like to think that the three-ghost tale of this novella serves as three parables illustrating how faith and self-transformation can change us from self-serving and insensitive people into caring, empathetic, and socially conscientious individuals. Or even better to consider how even good-natured folks like ourselves can be transformed into even better people of courage, dignity, and generosity. These three spirits of past, present, and future in Scrooge's nocturnal odyssey, I believe, advance the Christian moral mandate of its gospel of generosity, universal love, and kindness to community, which became a distinctive feature of the modern view of Christmas as endorsed by Dickens in Victorian England. I believe that this Christmas tale has less to do with solemn religious rituals but rather celebrates the joyous festivities of singing carols, sharing gifts with heartfelt greetings, and having festive celebrations around the family table enshrined by laughter and storytelling of past Christmases. This tale is about the bonding of families and communities not just at Christmas but also ever present in the humdrum ordinariness of life. And so this message of self-determination, faith, transformation, and self-giving voiced by *A Christmas Carol* is relevant for all times, for all places, and for all cultures.

Arguably, Dickens's most famous story is said to have had the greatest impact on Christmas celebrations in the Western world. The story's focus on the triumph of good over evil and the importance of family brought a new meaning to Christmas in the Victorian era and established the modern interpretation of Christmas as a festive family holiday. There were no Christmas cards in 1843 England, no Christmas trees at royal residences, no Christmas turkey dinners, no department-store Santa, no "yuletide" greetings, no gift-giving tradition or holiday lighting extravaganzas, no weeklong cessation of business affairs through the New Year, and no plethora of midnight services celebrating the birth of the Savior, for the holiday was relatively a minor affair that ranked far below Easter.[5]

The Dickens scholar Paul Davis comments about the novelty and significance of *A Christmas Carol.*

*A Christmas Carol* inverts the traditional folktale process. Instead of beginning as an oral story that is finally written down and formalized, Dickens's story has worked the other way. His story entered the world as a fully formed "perfect" work, and in the century and a half since its arrival, its original self has exploded like a sun into a supernova. Its hundreds and thousands of adaptations and productions—all those retellings and "re-originations"—have transformed a work of literature into the DNA of Western culture. "Disguised as Lionel Barrymore or Mister Magoo, Scrooge has become common cultural property and is deeply embedded in our consciousness as George Washington or Dick Whittington, Merlin or Moses." It is probably the secret dream of many writers to produce a work with such enduring power and is one of the several conundrums of the writing life that one can never live to see how it all turns out.[6]

I think the old saying "Comedy is tragedy plus time" applies to this story of an old miserable miser. Ebenezer Scrooge's spiritual blindness and lack of faith in humanity as he conducted his business with apathy toward others, together with his blatant disregard for Christmas, were his personal tragedy. However, with the passage of time as symbolized by Scrooge's dreams mirroring his missed opportunities in life, that resulted in a new life vision for Scrooge. The miserable miser now has been transformed into a man of faith in humanity with a new appreciation of the human virtues of goodness, empathy, and generosity. *A Christmas Carol* has been transformed from the tragedy of a miserable miser to a universal festive comedy. Throughout time, this tale lives on with its comedic characters with all their idiosyncrasies and eccentricities.

We can mimic and ridicule them for their eccentric ways just like how Fred Scrooge with his Christmas dinner guests found pleasure in mimicking the idiosyncrasies of "Uncle Scrooge" as that "loveable humbug."

In Dickens's masterwork of nonfiction, *A Christmas Tree* (1850), he sets out in his blend of essays, reminiscences, and takes an enthusiastic praise of life by articulating the great depth of his feelings for the Christmas season. He does this by conveying the same blend of childhood wonder, fantasy, humor, celebration, and solemnity, which distinguished *A Christmas Carol* among his many other Christmas tales.

Les Standiford describes very succinctly in his book *The Man Who Invented Christmas* how Dickens used the tree as perennial symbol of Christmas festivities, which we have admired to this very day.

Dickens closes his piece (of his work—*A Christmas Tree*) with a reminder of the tree as the centerpiece of the season's celebratory nature: "Now, the tree is decorated with bright merriment, and song and dance, and cheerfulness. And they are welcome. Innocent and welcome be they ever held, beneath the branches of the Christmas Tree, which cast no gloomy shadow!" *Dickens then adds a postscript*—"But as it sinks into the ground, I hear a whisper going through the leaves. 'This, in commemoration of the law of love and kindness, mercy and compassion. This, in remembrance of Me!'" And in reference to the words of Jesus and the Eucharist, he ties together the holy reason for the celebration and the acts of celebration itself. Though the clergy of the Anglican Church might be troubled by the concept of a Christmas tree as sacrament, for Dickens, it was the perfect union of the cloister and the hearth.[7]

The house on Devonshire Terrace where Dickens wrote *A Christmas Carol* is gone. So, too, the blacking house where Dickens worked endless hours where he tied tops to tiny pots of boot polish to support his family. Dickens too is gone but not forgotten, for as each Christmas comes, this immutable eternal story lives on.

On an unseasonably warm autumn evening in 1843, at a lavishly spacious apartment at 1 Devonshire Terrace, London, Charles John Huffam Dickens, at the age of thirty-one, began writing one of his many Christmas stories. In fact, he published more than a dozen Christmas short stories between 1835 and 1848. Besieged by writer's block after having three consecutive notable flops (*The Life and Adventures of Martin Chuzzlewit*, *Barnaby Rudge: A Tale of the Riots of 'Eighty'*, and *American Notes for General Circulation*), Dickens failed to get financial backing from his publishers, Chapman and Hall, for subsequent writings. This was an unfortunate state of affairs since Dickens was beginning to be regarded and admired in London as the "Shakespeare of the novel" and esteemed spokesman of the people as a champion of social reform. Possibly, Dickens's early fall from grace into hard times was due to his own presumptuous attitude resulting from his overnight success from 1837 to 1841 due to his renowned works of *The Pickwick Papers*, *The Life and Adventures of Nicholas Nickleby*, *The Old Curiosity Shop*, and culminating with *The Adventures of Oliver Twist*, which was celebrated in his first tour of America in 1842. Dickens was awestruck by how America accepted his works. He loved the friendliness and warmheartedness of America despite his criticism of many American ways, including America's table manners, his disappointment of the South's intolerance on the slavery issue, criticism of America's rigid prison system and the country's lack of enthusiasm for the arts and literature in deference to pursuing the "mighty dollar." All this along with the American piracies of books by foreign authors, disrespecting copyright laws left a bitter taste in his mouth. Dickens composed a travelogue of these criticisms of his visit, which became known as *The American Notes for General Circulation*, which was not received well in America. Dickens concluded his six-month vacation in the US with a stop in Canada where he appeared in light comedies in Niagara Falls, Toronto, Kingston, and Montreal. Returning from that trip, Dickens remarked to his good friend and literary adviser John Forster, "Americans are friendly, earnest, hospitable, frank, kind, fervent, accomplished, warmhearted and enthusiastic but I can't wait to return home."[8]

Dickens's return to Manchester, England, in October of 1843 to attend the Manchester Athenaeum for a speaking engagement to raise money for this philanthropic organization was an "eye-opener" and turning point for him. The city he once admired and loved for its promotion of learning, and the literary arts, he now abhorred, only to discover the deplorable work conditions of its cotton mills where unemployment in the mills hovered between 15 and 20 percent, and wages dropped precipitously.[9] Beyond his personal worries, he was keenly attuned to the profound misery of the working poor in this industrial city, which motivated him to tell the story of a greedy businessman Ebenezer Scrooge, who became one of the most famous characters in English literature. It was at this time in Manchester that convinced him that he needed to confront the problems of *want* and *ignorance*—the struggle of the haves and the have-nots that was rampant in the slums of England's newly industrial cities. This may have been the impetus of his Christmas novella and other ghost stories, which interestingly enough personified *want* and *ignorance* as the children of the Spirit of Christmas Present in his monumental short story. Dickens's need to highlight the income gap in Victorian England was the motivation for not only this Christmas novella but many of his novels as well.

Dickens proclaimed the day at Manchester with his speech at the Athenaeum as the origin of his eternal conviction that with the pursuit and accumulation of knowledge, one had the capacity to change oneself and one's lot in life, for the more one learns, the better and kinder one becomes. Self-transformation is possible through education and the discipline of the arts. His undying concern was to be the nation's voice to combat the evils of London's society of being insulated from and indifferent toward the two evils of want and ignorance, and most of all ignorance, which polarized the economic classes in England.

This certainly was a common theme in his works. He conveyed in his address in Manchester his most passionate belief—championing education, decrying ignorance and those who sought to perpetuate it, affirming a belief in the possibility of an individual's capacity of self-determination that fuels debate among social theorists in the day.[10]

With his current calamity of a troubled marriage having four children to support, with another child on the way, along with his career tottering headed for bankruptcy with beggar's prison in sight, Dickens desperately sought some respite by completing this Christmas novella, which is the subject of our discussion. Interestingly enough, he was able to complete the novella in a matter of six weeks from October through November of 1843. The festivities of Christmas were the last thing on his mind as he frequently took hours-long nighttime walks around London to seek inspiration and exhilaration in composing this work to ward off insomnia as he agonized to create the characters to battle writer's block.

Many of these characters were reflective of the personalities that he encountered in his own life and from the out-of-the-way places he frequented during these long evening walks in London. Crestfallen at the decision of his publishers Chapman and Hall declining his work, he made the bold decision to use what little funds he had to finance the costs of the book's production and also oversee the book's design, hire an illustrator, and consult on its advertising. In essence, his publishers—which would receive a fixed commission tied to its sales—had become merely his printer. In contemporary terms then, *A Christmas Carol* was to be an exercise in vanity publishing.[11] Little did he know this work would not only be an immediate success but be perennially commemorated in the world of literature as one of the finest holiday classics to this very day. Dickens's solitary evening walks through London's streets often ended after 15–20 miles, seeking inspiration needed to complete the work as soon as possible because of his dire financial situation. Dickens would trek through the darkest, dreariest corners of the city. It is with these evening walks where Dickens began to own up to and confront his inner conflicts and demons.

Samantha Silva in her novel *Mr. Dickens and His Carol* eloquently and cleverly personifies Dickens's inner struggles by describing his encounters with the mysterious Eleanor Lovejoy.[12] Dickens' transformation both as a human being and as an author is personified by his evening walk encounters with this fictitious beautiful young woman who worked as a seamstress for the local theater. He finds himself enthralled by her quiet nature and apparent understanding of his dilemma. Eleanor tested Dickens's preconceived beliefs about the goodness of humanity, generosity, friendship, ambition, and love.[13] Ironically, what Dickens naively took for granted about the goodness of human nature was challenged by Eleanor Lovejoy. This encounter speaks of the inner struggle Dickens had to reconcile his optimistic view of the goodness of humanity with the dark side of human selfishness, greed, and indifference. The result was he became a transformed person and regained his creativity as an author who achieved self-redemption despite all those vices, which haunted him while he experienced writer's block. According to Ms. Silva, Eleanor Lovejoy served as Dickens's muse in composing his Christmas tale. Lovejoy becomes that personification of Dickens's determination "to look into the mirror" and be introspective about his inner demons, which up to this point hampered his ability to write freely so as to be liberated of all those who wanted "a piece of him," causing him to be emotionally constrained and beleaguered.[14]

It is my opinion, like Lovejoy in Silva's novel, the character of Ebenezer Scrooge emerged as a personification resulting from Dickens's repressed inner struggles due to the lack of trust in his relationships with family, publishers, business colleagues, and the loves of his life. The transformation of Dickens as human being and author is personified in the process of transformation of the character of Ebenezer Scrooge. Scrooge, initially viewed as antagonist in the course of the tale, now becomes the protagonist of his Christmas story. This all came about as a result of Dickens's frequent night walks in London. His repressed inner struggles took the persona of a miserable, greedy, self-righteous, arrogant, and egotistical miser.

There is an interesting parallel and paradox of both characters of Lovejoy and Scrooge. Dickens later realizes stunningly that Lovejoy was merely a ghost, not a real person. All this made him realize how real she seemed to him more than anyone he had ever known. This all sprung from his imagination and his roiling conscience to achieve personal redemption. So too, the parallel of Dicken's character of Ebenezer Scrooge awakens from his ghost dreams to realize that he is real and has the power to change from being self-absorbed to being a genuine, self-giving, and a faith-filled individual. This insight allows him to attain the power to resolve his inner conflicts and alleviate self-pride, greed, and social indifference. Like his character Scrooge, Dickens had these inner conflicts, which fueled his lack of trust in humanity and detoured his goal for personal redemption as an author that were now resolved. Both fictitious characters Lovejoy and Scrooge in a sense become muses for Dickens, which transformed him to become a social conscience reformer.

This entire psychological and ethical process undergone by Dickens materialized into a novella, which would say much about faith in humanity, conversion, self-transformation, and human redemption. This message would evolve from a simple Christmas tale to a universal moral imperative for society.

This novella was published by Dickens with his own resources on December 19, 1843, originally entitled *A Christmas Carol, In Prose: Being a Ghost Story of Christmas*. It was completed in five chapters called staves. Its first edition sold out by Christmas Eve that year and became forever known as *A Christmas Carol*. Its success at least for a time delayed his financial woes despite the fact that earlier editions of this work didn't produce large profits. However, in the words of Les Standiford, who authored *The Man Who Invented Christmas* (2008), *A Christmas Carol* rescued Dickens's career and revived our holiday spirits. This novella presented a fresh outlook of the Christmas festival, which eventually became a major national celebration.

During the Victorian era of nineteenth-century England, authors such as Dickens were compensated by local publishers not only for their creativity and public appeal but also for the expediency to meet unrealistic deadlines for publication and compensated according to the length of their works. This may have been the reason why many of Dickens's works especially his fifteen novels were voluminous and also a reason why he prolifically authored five novellas, hundreds of short stories, nonfiction articles, and a handful of plays. His novels were initially serialized in weekly and monthly journals, then reprinted in standard book formats. "This format set the bar for serial publications of narrative fiction, which became the dominant Victorian mode for novel publication."[15]

Many of Dickens's works as reflected in *A Christmas Carol* highlighted the human virtue of faith in humanity and became an inspiration of how self-determination and self-transformation are redemptive of the human person. Dickens considered this particular short story, *A Christmas Carol,* one of the perfect examples of his conviction that the world could be a better and kinder place due to human determination. Dickens was criticized for his work by many puritans because he painted Christmas as a time for merrymaking and because he mentioned the believed demon liquor just a few many times in the story and was criticized for his blasphemy and flippant references to God sprinkled throughout the text.[16] All in all, Dickens breathed new life in the popular holiday of Christmas and restored it to its rightful place among human festivities, which had fallen into disfavor in Victorian England where puritanism had undermined the spiritual renewal of human existence. This along with the ill effects of the Industrial Revolution demeaned the value of human labor, propagated child labor, and diminished the dignity of the human person. The spiritual message of universal celebration of life, charity toward humanity, forgiveness for past transgressions, highlighting family loyalty, conversion of heart, and hope for a better future allows us to give a deaf ear to the criticisms this work received by the residual fringes of puritanism in London at that time.

*A Christmas Carol,* like many of his works, was an autobiographical sketch of Dickens's own family's experiences in childhood. Debtors' prison for Dickens was always in plain sight, resulting from his own financial woes and evident by his own father's spendthrift ways. This projection of gloom and doom became a catalyst for Dickens's lifelong devotion by bringing notice and giving voice to the underserved and the underprivileged in society through his writings. This was surely evident from his own childhood where his father, John, was forced by his creditors into Marshalsea debtors' prison in Southwark, London, in 1824. In order to avoid complete bankruptcy, his mother, Elizabeth, along with his entire family, including his youngest brothers and sisters, accompanied his father, John, to beggars' prison. In those days, it was customary that an entire family would accompany the debtor to prison. All this occurred while Charles at the age of twelve had to postpone his formal education for three years to work at Warren's Blacking Factory ten hours a day to tie covers to pots, then pasted the labels in order to support his own family.

Charles and his youngest sister, Frances (known to him as Fan), when free from her studies at the Royal Academy of Music, would spend Sundays with him visiting the family at Marshalsea. Fan was able to escape the family's financial woes by marrying an upright and religious gentleman. The character of Tiny Tim makes his way into the tale as personified in real life by little Henry, who was Dickens's nephew and Fan's son who was crippled and sickly.

Dickens describes the loneliness of his early days, which deepened his despair—"No advice, no counsel, no encouragement, no consolation, no support, from any one that I can call to mind, so help me God. I know I lounged about in the streets, insufficiently and unsatisfactorily fed. I know that, but for the mercy of God, I might easily have been, for any care that was taken of me, a little robber or a little vagabond."[17] Oddly enough, that personal sentiment would play out in his character of Oliver Twist. This childhood experience without a doubt was crucial for Dickens's entire future both as an author and a social reformer.

"It is hardly fanciful to say that in the blacking warehouse that unhappy child died, and into his frail body entered the spirit of a man of relentless determination…deep within…he would let nothing stand between him and ambition for he would batter his way out of all the 'gaols' that confine the human spirit."[18] The seeds of self-transformation and self-determination were already planted as he sought to work and forfeit his formal education at this time to contribute to getting his family released from Marshalsea.

It was from that day on that Dickens's self-determination became both his motivation and inspiration for authors in England to advocate for social reform to enlighten the minds and hearts of the prosperous and powerful in society to tend to the poor and powerless. This became a primary focus of Dickens's literary career. Social reform became the platform for most of his works. It was to commence with *The Adventures of Oliver Twist* (1838) and continue with *A Christmas Carol* (1843) until his final unfinished work of *The Mystery of Edwin Drood* (1870) due to Dickens suffering a stroke, which eventually took his life.

Like for any individual or for that matter any era in history, faith and self-transformation of the human person are shaped and influenced by the social environment of the day. In Dickens's day, this was no less the case for the writing of the *A Christmas Carol*, which was a product of Dicken's London in the early part of the nineteenth century.

Dickens's recollections of London began at the age of ten when he left his childhood home in Chatham, Kent, in 1822 and joined his parents in Camden Town, leaving to finish the school term traveling to London alone. The family house in Bayham Street, Camden Town, was not the house he imagined. It lay in one of those dismal suburbs, which was spreading even farther outward from Regency London. The population of London had already risen to well over a million when Dickens arrived with his family in Bayham Street. At one end of Camden Town stood the gloomy almshouses backing into a burial ground and the other where a lonely street began where there were run-down eating houses with a stretch of wasteland of rank grass and rubbish dumps, nettles, and duckweed. It was a far cry of the magical city that Charles envisioned London to be and what his character David Copperfield had imagined. Dickens many times referred to London as the "magic lantern" giving inspiration for his writings. London was not merely a backdrop but an inspiration of the city he loved, and the character of this city shaped many of the characters, incidents, and locations of his writings. In a letter to his good friend in 1846, Dickens wrote concerning London, "A day in London sets me up and starts me, but outside of the city the toil and labour of writing day after day without that magic lantern is immense!"[19]

There were frowzy fields, cowhouses, and dung hills and dust heaps and ditches everywhere. This was the kind of London landscape that Dickens had first known as a child. Charles was not sent back to school after his arrival at Camden Town, having to look after his younger brothers and sisters and taking on various errands to assist his family's poverty-stricken condition. It is here that he developed a habit for walking the streets of London, which later became his passion, which was the source of inspiration for many of his writings. Shortly after Charles's twelfth birthday, his father, John, came into an inheritance from his deceased mother, allowing him to pay off his debtors and so leave Marshalsea. Charles returned to school at Wellington House Academy in Camden Town.

Dickens procured a job as an office-boy to a firm experiencing the dark, dirty places smelling of must and dust and unwholesome sheep, a smell 'referable to the nightly and often daily consumption of mutton fat in candles, and to the fretting of parchment forms and skins in greasy drawers', to government offices, stationers' shops and legal chambers where 'the dull cracked windows in their heavy frames' have a 'determination to be always dirty and always shut', to clerks who sit on high stools with quill pens behind their ears and seem to spend their time—if old—in wearily scratching away in crumbling ledgers, or—if young—in mixing seidlitz powders, lolling over their desks on which their initials have been carefully carved, and in relating their experiences of the previous evening at the oyster shop, the cider cellar, the music hall or theatre.[20]

This was the dire environment Dickens experienced at a young age, which found its way into many of the descriptions of places, characters, storylines, and the "nooks and crannies" of his works.

Victorian London in Dickens's time featured homes of the upper class and middle class existing in close proximity to areas of immense poverty and filth. Rich and poor alike were thrown together in crowded streets. Street sweepers' major occupation was to keep streets clean of horse manure as a result of the heavy traffic of horse-drawn vehicles.

The atmosphere seemed to be smoldered in soot from thousands of chimney pots belching coal smoke, which seemed to settle everywhere. In many parts of the city, raw sewage flowed in gutters that emptied into the Thames River. The result of this was a massive stench hovering over the city and several outbreaks of cholera. While the Thames River provided commerce and wealth during the Industrial Revolution in London, it also brought death and disease. Jumping from one of London's bridges was a popular method of suicide as Dickens described the Thames in his novel *Little Dorrit* as "a deadly sewer," a harbinger of death and disease. London was besieged by pickpockets, prostitutes, drunks, beggars, and vagabonds, which added to the street vendors hawking their wares, which became a cacophony of street noises, which all found a place in Dickens's novels. This was the London Dickens knew.

After the Stage Carriages Act of 1832 in London, the hackney cab was replaced by the omnibus as a means of moving about the city.

These horse-drawn buses were carrying five hundred million passengers a year. All this added up to an incredible and intolerable amount of manure, which had to be removed from the streets. In wet weather, which occurred frequently, straw was scattered in walkways, storefronts, and in carriages to soak up the mud and water, but the stench remained. Cattle were driven through the streets. Dickens makes reference to them in *Oliver Twist*, describing the scene as Oliver and Bill Sikes travel through the Smithfield live-cattle market on their way to burglarize the Maylie home. The magic lantern city of Dickens's dreams had become the city of the great stink, alerting Parliament to take action in 1858 to address the terrible stench of the Thames River.

Until the second half of the nineteenth-century London, residents were drinking from the same parts of the Thames that open sewers were discharging into. This resulted in both the stench and cholera. The Broad Street pump was contaminated with raw sewerage coming from homes of cholera victims. It wasn't until Joseph Bazalgette, chief engineer of the new Metropolitan Board of Works (1855), put into effect a plan for a filtration system and an adequate sewerage system in 1875, preventing companies that supplied London's drinking water from drawing water from the most heavily tainted parts of the Thames.

The Victorian answer to dealing with the poor and indigent was the New Poor Law enacted in 1834. Previously, it was the burden of the parishes to care for the poor. The new law required parishes to band together and create regional workhouses where aid could be applied for. Eventually, these workhouses became no more than prisons for the poor. Civil liberties were denied, families were separated, and human dignity was destroyed. So in the words of the two portly unnamed solicitors describing the horrendous conditions of prisons and workhouses in London requesting provisions for the poor and destitute from Ebenezer Scrooge, "many can't go there; and many would rather die" were engraved in the opening section of the novella. To which Scrooge responds with a familiar line from *A Christmas Carol*, "If they would rather die, they had better do it and decrease the surplus population."

Charles Dickens, because of his childhood trauma caused by his father's imprisonment for debt and his own consignment to Warren's Blacking Factory to help support his family, was a true champion of the poor.

He repeatedly pointed out the atrocities of the system through his novels. It was through works such as *A Christmas Carol* and other popular novels that many of the ills of nineteenth-century London were remedied through education, technology, and social reform.

It was with the growing social consciousness empowered by his works that by the turn of the century, with the death of Queen Victoria in 1901, the Victorian period came to a close and that advocacy for the common person and the poor now had a voice in their future. Thus, Dickens's dream for a better London and a return to London as "the magic lantern" could become a reality.

There are five major themes in the novella, which reflect the impoverished state of London in Dickens's lifetime, which contributes to the genesis of this Christmas tale. The first is the urgency caused by time. The dreamlike state created by Dickens to introduce us to the events of Ebenezer Scrooge's past, present, and future undertakings becomes the heart of this novella. Each time sequence is identified with a spirit that moves the story along: the flame glowing light of the spirit of the past, the greater-than-life-size Giant Saint Nick characterized by the spirit of the present, and the dark, faceless, and hooded creature with bony fingers pointing to the future. Scrooge's time as Marley's ghost had accentuated at the outset of the story is growing short. While there is still time remaining, Scrooge needs to reform his life so as not to suffer the same fate of Marley, whose life sentence was to wander the world in an endless purgatory. At the same time, the sequence of each ghost appearance highlights that life is passing Scrooge by with the ultimatum—what will happen after Scrooge's death if he continues down the path of greed and avarice, resulting in the exploitation of people?

The passage of time is captured by its many sounds—first, bells tolling and chiming, reminding Scrooge that his time is passing and his life is spent. The clanging sound of chains that Marley shakes to frighten Scrooge prior to the ghost appearances are a reminder of the urgency that Scrooge faces the same fate as Marley unless he reforms his current sinful life. Time also becomes an ugly reminder of all the cultural changes occurring in London at this time due to the Industrial Revolution, which threaten to break down long family traditions many times, resulting in impending poverty within the socioeconomic structure of Victorian England.

Secondly, the cohesiveness of the family unit was challenged as symbolized by the coldness, loneliness, and indifference exhibited by the story's antagonist Ebenezer Scrooge, who is opposed to the intimacy of family life. This is characterized by his empty hearth, keeping his place of business poorly lit and poorly heated for his clerk and sole employee, Bob Cratchit, in order to save money. Scrooge also shrugs off his nephew Fred's Christmas greetings with "a bah humbug," denouncing the merriment of Christmas. Scrooge's only "friend" was Jacob Marley, who was solely a business partner rather than a genuine friend with no other purpose than they share their lives together as bachelors and the suite of rooms for merely business purposes.

Thirdly, greed, generosity, and forgiveness all seemed to be embroiled in a combatant struggle in the perennial battle of good versus evil. Greed was the center of Scrooge's existence, which caused him to lose his fiancée, his family, and his respect from the townspeople. Dickens utilized his own appreciation of family values to engineer the story so that Scrooge becomes more aware of his morally impoverished life. Progressively, as the story unfolds, Scrooge learns to be remorseful and repentant so as to be in tune with his buried conscience so that he could see goodness and virtue in others. This insight leads him ultimately to his redemption.

Fourthly, the attraction of future generations in reading *A Christmas Carol* comes from the intrigue of the genre of the ghost story, which is basically a moral tale proven timeless because it was designed to expose the social issues of Victorian London. It would eventually be applicable for other cultures in Europe and future eras where human rights and freedoms were violated. Dickens makes use of the seasonal period around Christmas with the cold, bleak winter weather to highlight the unfairness and pain experienced by the terribly impoverished families of this time and how the current laws, policies, and economic system of London's society overlooked their plight.

The repetition of Scrooge's distinctive phrase *humbug* throughout is a symbol of that insensitivity, ignorance, and inequality where he dismissed the poor and those whom society marginalized. We learn that Scrooge is the most impoverished character lacking love, human compassion, and ultimately the spirit of Christmas. Scrooge is remedied in the story by his nephew Fred and his employee Bob Cratchit along with his loving family who demonstrate to Scrooge the true meaning of goodness, faithfulness, and intimacy of family life. Even though those who surround Scrooge are financially downtrodden, they do succeed in challenging Scrooge's lifestyle, which triggers an inner catharsis, causing him to forsaken his greed and replace it with humility and love.

Finally, Christmas and the Christian tradition are given a new outlook by linking them together to the extent that the religious meaning of Christmas celebrating the birth of the Christ Child could be integrated with festivities of caroling, family dinners, dance, and music.

Dickens used the term *staves* instead of chapters as a metaphor for a simple song with a beginning, middle, and end to use the idea of singing carols to connect this tale to joyful Christian traditions of the season.

It is the festive Christmas atmosphere that flourished in the streets along with the ethos of the nativity narrative, which is embodied in the characters like Tiny Tim, Bob Cratchit, and Fred Scrooge who are the living embodiment of goodness, generosity, and kindness. Christmas served Dickens's purpose to show how Scrooge's transformation and ultimate redemption as processed in his dream parables would appeal to readers' Christianity as well in an effort to change a society that was structured in ways that he saw as being profoundly un-Christian.

# Faith—a Many Splendored Mystery

I wear the chain I forged in life, I made it link by link, yard by yard;
I girded it on of my own free will, and of my own free will I wore it.
—Jacob Marley

There was a popular song in the early 1960s called "Love Is a Many Splendored Thing," which won the Academy Award in 1955 for the best original song. It received acclaim by one of America's favorite singers Andy Williams in 1962. If we substitute the word *faith* for *love* in the following lyrics of the song, it defines what faith brings to human life.

Love [Faith] is a many-splendored thing
Its's the April rose that only grows in the early spring
Love [Faith] is nature's way of giving a reason to
    be living
the golden crown that makes a man a king
Once on a high and windy hill, in the morning mist
Two lovers kissed and the world stood still

> Then your fingers touched my silent heart and
> taught it how to sing
> Yes, true love [faith] is a many splendored thing[21]

Faith is indeed a many splendored and multifaceted reality. Like love, faith is not a thing but a relationship. Faith is a human-inherent drive for life. "Faith is the assurance of things hoped for; the conviction of things not visibly seen" (Hebrews 11:1).[22] It is the "stuff" that believing is made of. It allows us to make decisions and to take ownership of our lives "link by link" and "yard by yard" by our own free will. It determines the ultimate consequences of our future. Faith, like love, is nature's way of giving us reason to be alive and gives rise to second chances.

Faith, similar to love, touches our hearts to believe in another human being. Faith finds its fulfillment in love as found in relationships and causes our world to pause so as to hear the voice of the Other. The Other may be a lover or the voice of God.

Faith involves the human act of believing. For it always involves the intimacy of relationship, for without relationship, faith doesn't exist.

The act of believing is visceral, meaning I invest my trust, my hopes, my aspirations, and ultimately my life in the hands of another person.

Believing is faith's first movement; it is the first step. Believing is always "believing in" another. If we were to look up the meaning of believing in the dictionary, it says "to lend credence to or hold to be true." Believing is an intimate, existential, dynamic, relational, and visceral human act. When a person promises me something or to perform a task, if I have trust in the person's words, it is as if I have already embraced the promised gift or completed the task agreed upon. When a trustworthy person tells me something that I cannot readily verify, it is through an act of trust in the person that I obtain knowledge of what has been communicated to me. Believing is intimate because it is personal, always involving relationship. It is existential because it involves the present, the here and now. It is dynamic because it triggers a field of trust between two individuals. It is relational because it always involves knowing and loving the Other and the Other reciprocating this transaction. Finally, believing is visceral because it has to do with the heart, not the mind.

Although believing gives rise to beliefs, beliefs are secondary in importance to the act of believing. Beliefs, whether religious, political, or philosophical, are at the service of living faith. It is "believing in" the Other, not solely beliefs that give rise to the lifestyle of faith. The lifestyle of faith is not a fashion statement or a crusade but a freely chosen human act. Faith is not earned, purchased, won, or owned but always a gift. Where believing has to do with what we are now, faith is the lifestyle of what we will be in the future. It always comes at a cost, not out of our pockets but from our hearts. Faith demands that "I must be willing to give up what I am in order to become what I will be."[23] Faith is that gift that has to be continually nurtured and loved into maturity. Faith is a life and, like a human being, can easily die from neglect.

Believing seeks the voice of faith to receive expression and allow for a language between humans so that relationship can happen. Faith is not only a virtue or an admirable human attribute but a life arising from relationships in real time. Faith is the primordial building block of relationships. It is the rock foundation when building a life.

In human terms, faith is that trust born of relationships where one becomes self-gift to another. In turn, faith is self-revelatory of who we are and gives foundation to our standing in the world. Faith is also redemptive and transformative, bringing out the best and goodness of ourselves to be shared with others. The hope of "believing in" will free us to experience all the goodness, energy, inspiration, and joy that money can't buy but what other human beings can provide. Faith's subjects are exclusively human beings in relationship or, as we shall explore later in this chapter, human beings in relationship with the Divine.

Whether these relationships are friendships, work-related, family-oriented, sexual, and intimate, couples in commitment or marriages nonetheless all are subject to what faith is. Faith has to do with questioning ourselves about our motivation and discovering who we are as human beings in relationship with others. It is being true to ourselves not by what others expect of us but by living the truth and seeking righteousness, justice, and peace. Faith has to do with believing that life is worth the work in living. Faith is only real and authentic when it is shared. Faith is not virtual but real and concrete. That is why it always involves relationship that is real and concrete.

Faith is not obsessed with "selfies" but to be responsible self-givers. Faith is an extension of oneself to another, which thrives to know and love and allows the Other to reciprocate the same expectation—to be known and be loved. It is not intellectually driven but driven by love. Faith is a life journey of the soul that seeks what is special in the human heart and is *par excellence* a human reality. When faith evolves into an endless drive that goes beyond oneself, seeking infinity and eternal life, it falls within the realm of divine mystery. For this reason, faith is a many splendored and multifaceted reality and interestingly enough a divine mystery.

*Faith as Human Reality*

The first movement to faith is the human act of believing. The act of believing is the antithesis of the unpredictable and fickle ways of the world. The world can be a cruel teacher. Believing initiates hope that life experiences can be good teachers and change one for the better. The world can change from moment to moment as we have witnessed in our struggles with dealing with a pandemic. On the other hand, believing is an anchored choice, which, when repeated over time, is what faith is about. Believing is the first step one takes in the present to live in faith as a lifetime journey. All the choices we make are linked with actions that either enhance faith or depart from it.

The first significant characteristic of faith on the human level is that *faith is the state of being ultimately concerned.*[24] Ultimate concern was the definition given to what faith is attributed to the twentieth-century theologian and philosopher Paul Tillich (1886–1965), who is considered the father of Christian existentialism.[25]

Ultimate concern means that faith is at the very heart of one's existence. Humanity has many concerns: cognitive, aesthetic, social, political, religious, economic, safety, and the pursuit of freedom, peace, and tranquility. Some of these concerns are urgent, oftentimes justifiable, and each of them can claim ultimacy for the life of society.

"If the concern claims ultimacy it demands the total surrender of one who accepts the claim, and it promises total fulfillment even if all other claims have to be subjected to it or rejected in its name."[26]

Tillich gives an example of viewing faith as one's ultimate concern.

If a national group of citizens make the life and development of their nation, i.e., nationalism, its ultimate concern, it demands that all other priorities are secondary—i.e., economics, politics, individual well-being, education, family life, aesthetic and cognitive truth, justice—and humanity be sacrificed for nationalism. Nationalism becomes the ultimate priority. Nationalism is "likened to a god" for its citizens.

I recall a case early in my clinical practice where a couple came to treatment struggling over intimacy issues largely because one of the partners was spending an inordinate amount of time and care for their elderly father who was a widower and lived alone. This time and care spent were at the expense of the other partner in the relationship.

This resulted in relationship estrangement over a period of five years where they experienced each other as strangers and no longer lovers. In this case, the patient made her father the object of her ultimate concern. This became a mortal blow not only to their relationship but also with her other priorities such as her career and her relationship with her friends. Although this is a negative example of the meaning of ultimate concern, it accentuates what the essential characteristic of what human faith is about.

Ultimate concern can be seen or rather seen by its omission in Dickens's character Jacob Marley. Marley, a character documented factiously by Dickens, who supposedly lived from March 8, 1783, to December 24, 1836, was the business partner of Ebenezer Scrooge. They had worked together as apprentices in the business of accounting. This accounting firm referred to in the novella was descriptive of how a nineteenth-century financial institution, probably a counting house, operated. Marley referred to their offices as "our money-changing hole." Both Marley and Scrooge became successful bankers with seats on the London Stock Exchange. Most of their wealth was accumulated through usurious moneylending. Scrooge was described by Dickens as Marley's sole executor, his sole administrator, his sole residuary legatee, his sole friend, and ultimately his sole mourner. The tale opens with mention of Marley's death seven Christmas Eves ago. Marley's indifference toward others made him an unpopular personality in town since he was solely dedicated to accumulating monetary gains. That was his ultimate concern. Or one could say his indifference toward the concerns of others was his lack of ultimate concern.

In Jacob Marley's case, his keen business sense along with his cleverness networking a partnership and a friendship with Scrooge produced large monetary gains. Their passion and self-indulgence to accumulate limitless wealth many times by exploiting others became their ultimate concern. Over time, Marley, like Scrooge, so indulged in greed and avarice that they drove Mr. Fezziwig, their mentor, to forfeit his business to them. This escalating pattern of greed many times by exploiting others did not enhance faith in humanity but forged a chain of self-destruction, eventually leading to perdition.

It is particularly interesting how Dickens illustrates Marley's ghost appearance, which opens the novella. Marley's ghost carries the concerns he had in life—the chain it carries is made of cash boxes, keys, padlocks, ledgers, deeds, and burdensome purses all made of steel. These items symbolize objects of Marley's ultimate concern in lieu of genuine relationships with people. His faith and security were based upon the accumulation and protection of his financial assets.

Marley is a bitter, greedy, and selfish human being and upon his death was cursed to eternally wander the earth as a decrepit spirit forever burdened by the mass chains, which represent his slavery to money.

One could claim that the sole redeeming factor of Jacob Marley was that Dickens uses him as a catalyst for initiating the process of Scrooge's conversion. Marley's apparition instills fear in Scrooge to the extent of being, in Scrooge's own words, a "terrible sensation." Marley's visit offers Scrooge a way out and a chance of redemption. This scene concludes where Marley's ghost leaves Scrooge and joins in a mournful dirge as it enters the bleak and dark night. Here Scrooge sees the air filled with phantoms, wandering in restless haste, moaning as they wander here and there aimlessly, and each wore a chain similar to Marley's ghost in an abode of misery and darkness. They were all seeking to interfere for the good in human matters, but they had lost their power to do so (stave 1—"Marley's Ghost"). The wailing and moaning of lifeless creatures, some of which Scrooge recognized in his current life, became Scrooge's terrible sensation and haunting image as he awaited the visits of the three spirits.

There is an amazing scene in the 1951 movie adaptation of *A Christmas Carol* (not in the original novella) starring Alastair Sim as Scrooge where Scrooge goes to visit Jacob Marley on his deathbed on Christmas Eve. As Scrooge bends over the dying Marley to hear his dying words, Marley, who hardly can speak, utters to Scrooge, "While there is still time…save yourself." Scrooge, oblivious to Jacob's dying words, responds, "Save myself… Save myself from what?"

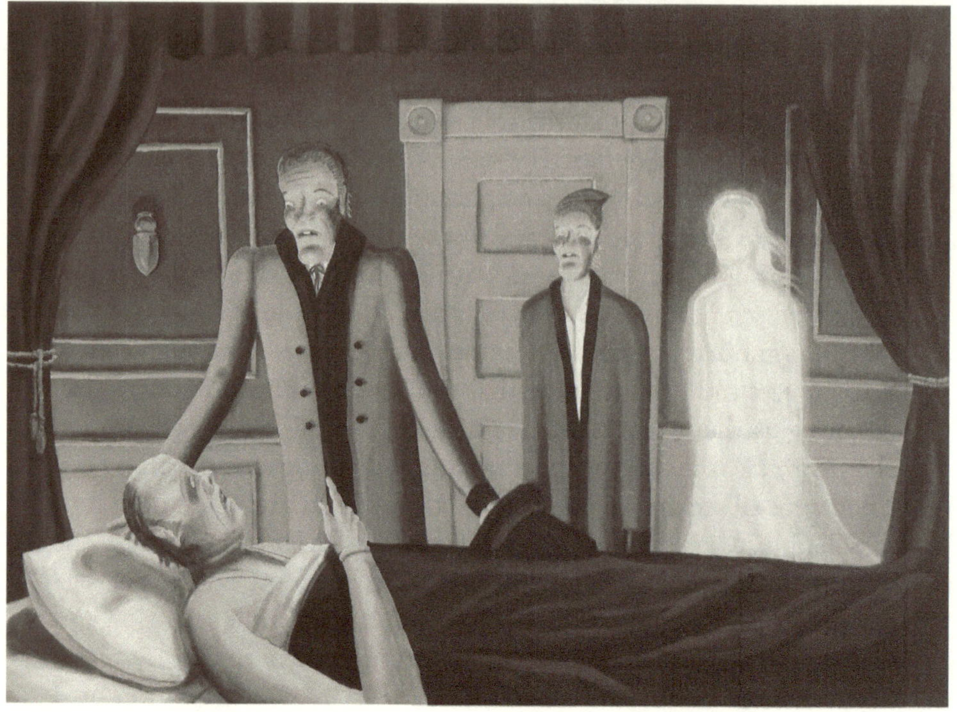

This sets the tone for the rest of the story as Scrooge begins his journey to find himself.

Faith in human relationship is all that Marley was not about.

He reveled in the luxury of wealth. He responded with apathy and indifference toward the well-being of humanity as demonstrated by his lack of social responsibility. Marley' sole relationship was with his love of money, which was both his life's goal and his ultimate concern. Marley's faith was solely in the power of money. The character of Jacob Marley is probably the only one in the novella who never discovers or appreciates what faith can bring to human existence. Marley is completely sour on the reality of faith as being transformative and salvific.

I do not wish to be so presumptuous to say that Marley lacked faith entirely since in his ghostly existence, he seems to demonstrate remorse of his self-centered earthly life by persuading Scrooge to avoid his fate by agreeing to meet the three spirits. I would contend that Marley's afterlife became a sort of purgatory in a restless search of faith, which he did not cherish during his earthly life. Only the Almighty can ultimately judge if Marley deserved eternal damnation, which goes beyond the scope of this Christmas tale.

What we can learn from Marley is the helplessness and emptiness he experienced at the end of life are in direct correlation to the fact that he couldn't accept others in faith. He never was able to participate in a transformation of life with the purpose to respect and acknowledge the dignity of others. This is Marley's sin that he never allowed faith in others to allow him to reach his highest potential as a human being but was content to just reap the monetary gains of his labor. In this sense, Marley is one to be pitied. It is safe to say that the Jacob Marleys of the world never really live life in serenity, peace, and tranquility since there is never enough wealth to satisfy their insatiable greed. They never get to experience the fruit of faith, which is to be loved by others.

The human reality of faith is always about encountering a genuine relationship with other human beings. To know and to love the Other and the acceptance of the reciprocity of being known and loved by the Other is the essence of what it means to be human. This is at the heart of relationship. This is what was missing in Jacob Marley's life and what he couldn't recapture in the afterlife. This is the essence of one's ultimate concern—to establish a genuine relationship with another. This is the beginning of the life of faith. Where there is no relationship, there is no faith. Where there is no faith, relationship is solely a shell of itself—an interaction with others solely for practical concerns.

If the first characteristic of faith involves one's ultimate concern, then it follows that ultimate concern is always in context of the relationship with the Other.

The second characteristic of faith as human reality is that it is an unconditional acceptance of the Other for all that the Other is.

Again, the Other is another human being or the Divine depending upon what context one speaks of faith. This unconditional acceptance of the Other is a dialogue of presence that says to the Other, "I am here in the present and accept you totally for who you are."

It is essentially being present for the Other, not necessarily doing for the Other. This dialogue of presence is bilateral and sheds light on each in the relationship to look at the truth about oneself with fortitude and honesty. The acceptance of the Other doesn't mean I need to agree with the convictions, lifestyle, or opinions or likes of the Other. It solely means that despite our differences and human needs, I stand with you with no questions asked. Acceptance entails trust. This trust is not only receiving something from another but also actually accepting the other as who the other is.

The unconditional acceptance of another involves one's love for another. Love is that unconditional acceptance of who one is not what lifestyle one has chosen. When people fail to notice one another or no longer have the time for one another, we begin to wonder about the quality of their love. It's difficult to ignore people and claim to love them at the same time. Awareness is a very important human disposition because it is the precondition of love. We can't love people we don't even notice. Love or unconditional acceptance presupposes awareness. So, too, love heightens our unconditional resolve to care for another since we pay attention not only to other but also with what is going on in their lives.

This becomes clearly evident in Scrooge's relationship with his first and only true love—his fiancée, Belle. The unconditional acceptance of the Other, in this case Belle, over the many years has dire consequences for Scrooge. It challenges him to reexamine and clarify his motivations and life's goals. Belle serves as Scrooge's wake-up call and invitation to embody faith in commitment. Scrooge needs to weigh his priorities and ultimate concern in making a choice either to accept faith in the relationship with Belle or to retreat into himself and seek his security elsewhere. As we discover, he finds that security elsewhere, which is his lust for wealth.

Scrooge and Belle had agreed to contract marriage when they were young and poor. Belle assertively tells Ebenezer that she has been displaced for a golden idol. She was extremely upset that she was replaced by his lust for wealth. She calls him out for forgetting his roots of how they both met as children of poor working-class families.

Belle reluctantly and heartbreakingly releases Ebenezer from his legally binding engagement to marry her to relieve him of any lawsuit for breach of contract. Belle dismisses Scrooge with the words, "May you be happy in the life you have chosen!" At this point, Scrooge recalls Marley's words referring to his burdensome chain where he now experiences incessant torture and remorse—it was a life Scrooge had chosen "link by link and yard by yard" of his own free will, and his own free will wore it. Scrooge could not respond in kind to the faith that Belle so placed in him and in their future life together. The unconditional acceptance of the Other, in this case the promise of marriage, was forsaken. Scrooge is now accountable to the truth about himself as he abandons his love of a person for a thing. Belle becomes that beacon of faith's light challenging Scrooge to reconsider what was his ultimate concern in life.

Ending his first dream sequence of Christmas past, Scrooge is brought by the light of the Spirit of Christmas Past to witness how Belle moved on with her life, marrying and enjoying her children with her husband. This is an experience that Scrooge could never fathom, having chosen wealth over his beloved. In fact, in this closing episode of the visit of the ghost of Christmas Past, Scrooge hears Belle's husband say to her that he clearly recalls that he saw an old friend, only to find that Scrooge's business was not closed up, but a candle was burning on his desk as Ebenezer sat alone, pondering and staring into the dark space of his office. Scrooge sat sadly alone as his partner Marley was at the point of death. Belle's husband reiterated that Scrooge sat alone with the candle on his desk and continued to be alone in the world. Scrooge wonders if this would have been his family with Belle. This causes him to wrestle with the spirit to conceal his light, which manifested this particular vision, saying, "Leave me! Take me back, haunt me no longer!" Scrooge wanted to extinguish the light as shown by the head of the first spirit. The spirit put up no resistance as the tale goes on to say the following:

> Scrooge observed that its light was burning
> high and bright; and dimly connecting that with

its influence over him, he seized the extinguish-
er-cap, and by a sudden action pressed it down
upon its head. The Spirit dropped beneath it, so
that the extinguisher covered its whole form; but
though Scrooge pressed it down with all his force,
he could not hide the light; which streamed from
under it, in an unbroken flood upon the ground.
(Stave 2—"The First of the Three Spirits")

Scrooge could not accept the truth of who he became without Belle, for he blocked the light of faith as symbolized by the flame of light over the head of the first spirit, which he attempted to extinguish.

He refused to let this light penetrate his heart so as to alter his life priorities. His promise for an unconditional relationship with Belle abruptly ended after many years of courtship. Scrooge's ultimate concern was not Belle but wealth.

The unconditional acceptance of the Other produces a dialogue of presence between two persons in an indelible bond of trust where words are not needed to communicate. It is a bond of heart to heart and soul to soul, which need not speak words. Each person feels the loyalty and commitment of each standing beside each other. This is what Belle aspired to and what Scrooge wasn't able to deliver because he made his ultimate concern the lust of wealth. Authentic human faith is always personal and deals with humans in relationship. In the dialogue of presence, which is the unconditional acceptance of another, there is no in between. Presence becomes an existential bond of souls created in relationship. The sole purpose of unconditional acceptance is being with the Other. It is only in this personal dialogue of two beings that both experience the height, the depth, the transparency, the harmony, and the mutuality of each other. It is not mental telepathy but rather a yearning for the good of the Other. It is here that each find oneself and therefore realizes one's standing with the world. It is in losing ourselves in the Other that we find ourselves. The best example of this is two human beings in love. The human presence, which is extremely powerful, needs not words. Sometimes when we try to find words to express something important to us, like how we felt when "we fell in love," we are speechless due to the limitations of language. As T. S. Eliot observed,

> It's strange that words are so inadequate.
> Yet, like the asthmatic struggling for breath
> So the lover must struggle for words.

We can conclude that human presence to another is the sole fabric and primary characteristic of human relationship. The closest metaphor I can think of to describe this dialogue of presence of the unconditional acceptance of the Other is that lovers who are present to each other are soul mates. They are distinct as individuals but unified in one heart, one mind, and one being without words or action. They are being for each other. Lovers look at each other without words but stand present in the here and now for each other. This is what human faith involves—a commitment of fidelity, loyalty, and self-giving. This is what Scrooge could not render to Belle or to any other human being for that matter.

A third characteristic of human faith is the act of reaching out to the Other in hope. This characteristic is more than mere charity but an attitude of extending empathy to the Other and showing interest and concern for the interests of the Other. This was best exemplified by the two nameless solicitors who approached Scrooge in the opening scene of the novella requesting funds for the poor and the destitute. It also was a disposition exhibited by Scrooge's nephew Fred, who visits his uncle Scrooge, wishing him a merry Christmas with an invitation to his home for Christmas dinner. Both extensions of empathy and kindness are met with the blatant Scrooge response, "Bah humbug." This term in colloquial Victorian England connoted a hoax, imposition, fraud, or sham, used interjectionally to mean "stuff and nonsense," in slang to deceive or cheat.[27] This was basically Scrooge's disposition not only toward Christmas but also to any situation where it was called upon of him to extend kindness to another for any purpose and in any circumstance.

In comparison to Scrooge's negative disposition to others' concerns, the unconditional aspect of faith as extending oneself as confidant reassurance is evident in the person of Bob Cratchit in the manner he relates to his own family—his wife and six children. In fact, how he acts toward whomever he encounters is the empathetic gentleman of hope. Faith as extending oneself as confidant reassurance of another's talents, trials, and tribulations is what it meant to be truly and unconditionally human. This is the essence of this third characteristic of faith as human reality—confidant reassurance of things unseen that we inspire and validate others to what they hold dear.

The manifestations of these unseen human realities of extension to others are compassion, loyalty, generosity, mercy, forgiveness, patience, kindness, empathy, rejoicing in another's success and happiness, and supporting in others' interests. All these define what love is. All these attributes define what faith is as confidant reassurance—hope. Faith gives rise to hope, and both culminate in love. All these define what is good about being human. Bob Cratchit becomes the anchor of hope for not only his family but also everyone he encounters. He empathizes with the two gentlemen who solicit funds for the poor. His jovial greeting in meeting Fred who comes to see his uncle Scrooge validates and joins in with Fred's festive sharing of the Christmas spirit. This gift of hope is also evident in Bob Cratchit's supportive approach with his wife attempting to ease her fears about the future of their son Tim's health condition.

> "And how did little Tim behave?" asked Mrs. Cratchit when she had rallied Bob on his credulity, and Bob had hugged his daughter [Martha] to his heart's content. "As good as gold," said Bob, "and better". Somehow, he gets thoughtful, sitting by himself so much, and thinks the strangest things you ever heard. He

told me, coming home, that he hoped the people saw him in church, because he was a cripple, and it might be pleasant to them to remember upon Christmas-day who made lame beggars walk and blind men see." Bob's voice was tremulous when he told them this, and trembled more when he said that Tiny Tim was growing strong and hearty. (Stave 3—"The Second of the Three Spirits")

Bob Cratchit's character is the apex of hope and the enemy of fear. For the enemy of both faith and hope in what potentially humans can accomplish is fear. In the renowned film series *Star Wars* by George Lucas, in the first episode titled "The Phantom Menace," the powerful progression of fear could not have been described better than Yoda, who says, "I sense a great disturbance in the 'force' of fear which turns to anger and then hate and finally suffering." Yoda—the fictitious ancient, powerful, and wise Jedi master—correctly defines the destructive power of all human fear, which results in anger, hatred, and lastly, suffering. Fear is the enemy of love. Hope is a cousin to faith, which counteracts fear and becomes the driving force of a vibrant faith in humanity. Faith without hope is an allusion; however, faith with hope is confidant reassurance. Hope is the constant reassurance of confidence that rests in not only being true to oneself but also always seeking the good for the Other whether convenient or inconvenient. Hope strives for those who make faith their ultimate concern in life because it fuels steadfast love in relationship with another person. Hope is the ultimate extension to the Other. Hope varies with a person's age, culture, health, and family circumstance. Hope is always at the heart of the human faith experience. Hope varies from person to person. It can induce one to be ambitious about one's future and yet at the same time be heroic. Hope can stir desires, plans, and aspirations. Hope can also make people fearful of their future at times or even selfish. However, what hope will do is to drive one to believe in the goodness of people and move others to faith. Again, hope is the ultimate extension of the heart to another. Whenever we hope in people, we strengthen their resolve and lessen their anxieties. If we sense that someone in need has hope in us, not just in what we can do for them but trust us dearly, this makes us gift givers like Bob Cratchit. This engenders trust and credibility in relationships.

The patient endurance of the giver of hope who is the person of faith risks everything. It is high stakes for the faith-filled person with a future that remains unclear and even unknown. When we hope in human beings, we are bound to what happens to them. We always run the risk of being taken for granted and being vulnerable. Hope is the key to the act of believing, which is the first step of a faith lifestyle. It makes the act of believing dynamic and existential. Dynamic in the sense that we will discover things about ourselves that we never realized by being vulnerable. Ultimately, we discover the power within, which contributes to making a difference in people's lives. Existentially in the sense that we trust in the here and now with no guarantee to be rewarded or compensated in the future. Those in need are moved viscerally by those who generously respond by being totally present to them; this is the dialogue of presence as we discussed before. Those in need despite their struggles in turn reciprocate by believing in the goodness of people who responded selflessly to them without question. Those in need are not the victims but receptors of the self-givers who become lifesavers and even more dramatic life changers. Believing is a bilateral dynamic experience, which is a catalyst for faith. Believing is in the present; faith is for the future. Faith fuels that hope whether blessed or cursed with the ability to face the fears of the future and respond courageously through action. Essentially, human beings cannot actualize themselves without the power of faith and the consistency of hope in someone so that life can be good, meaningful, and worthwhile.

Faith involves personal choice to be gift givers of hope. It involves believing that being present totally to others is not just a "Christmas thing" but the difference between life and death. Faith needs to be relational and grounded in the community of humanity, for no one is an island unto themselves, nor does anyone alone have all the answers to life's challenges. We have unfortunately learned this the hard way through the horrific experiences brought to our doorstep by the recent pandemic.

A concrete example of the hope we give to others because of our faith in humanity can be seen in the legendary novel *Of Mice and Men* by John Steinbeck. I recall reading this novel for the first time as required summer reading when I was a sophomore in high school.

In the novel, the character Crooks, a black disabled farmhand, is alienated by other farmhands because of the color of his skin and also complicated by the fact that he couldn't do the work they did because of his disability. This fueled the ire of the rest of the workers since he was also paid but relegated to taking care of his boss's living quarters and office. Crooks attempts to convince Lennie Small, a mentally challenged farmhand, that everyone needs to trust in at least one person in their life no matter how much or what one knows. Crooks attempts to quell Lennie's fears that his partner and best friend, George, will not stray or abandon Lennie despite George not getting in touch with him for days. George had gone into town to gamble. Crooks, who spent much of his time in his boss's office reading his employer's books, says to Lennie, "Books ain't no good. A guy needs someone to talk to him because life gets too lonely. It can make a guy sick."

Trust is that lifeline that keeps faith alive. Again, trust is not so much about what another person gives me or what I give to another but acceptance of the other person for who they are. It is putting our life in the hands of another. This is where faith cries out for relationship. Hope provides that fertile ground that makes believing possible. Relationship needs to be the medium of the human empowerment that we call faith. Humanity cries out for relationships with other humans. Faith needs human relationships. Human relationships need faith.

Hope keeps faith alive. Hope is that human extension and reaching out, embracing concern, empathy, and interest in another human life.

A fourth characteristic of faith as human reality is the drive to be grounded in truth, justice, and righteousness. Faith without knowledge is blind; however, faith with knowledge is wisdom. Faith without wisdom is myth; however, faith with wisdom is enlightenment. Faith is grounded in common sense, not in individual whim or opinion. Faith is governed by what is true and good, not what is treasured by popular demand. Faith is believing without the evidence always vulnerable to doubt and one's biases. The risk we take to exercise faith is human doubt.

Human doubt doesn't negate faith but challenges and strengthens our resolve to belief and hold it to the test of reality.

Although truth is grounded in knowledge, knowledge alone is not the source of faith. Knowledge is needed for faith to seek understanding of the human condition, its expectations, and its goals. Knowledge is needed to allow faith to develop and be expressed in language for a culture. Faith transcends the language of doctrine, creed, and goes beyond the world of beliefs, which are conditioned by time and history. One doesn't necessarily need knowledge to attain faith, but knowledge validates the one who has faith. Knowledge along with faith can pursue truth.

The goal of faith is justice and righteousness. Faith is the prerequisite for demonstrating justice for all. It is not enough to believe that all human beings are entitled to justice. Justice needs to be exhibited in our behavior where we treat humanity with dignity, respect, and equality. There is no love without justice. Faith holds justice to the sacred belief that all human lives matter. Righteousness means that we make our human choices not solely based exclusively from knowledge attained or solely based upon our good intentions or exclusively on our emotions but on the universal premise that all human life is precious, sacred, and is deserving of dignity and protection. Many times, we need faith to make choices even when we don't have all the knowledge or all the answers or despite our good intentions or because it makes us feel good. We need to make righteous choices because it is the right thing to do despite our knowledge, good intentions, or emotions. It may not be the popular or "politically correct" thing to do but the morally right thing to do. This is what righteousness means in terms of acting in faith. Righteousness establishes a balance of what I am able to do and what I must do. Righteousness means that faith needs to be translated into good works. Faith without healthy, good, and responsible behavior is empty. Truth, justice, and righteousness all work together to ensure that my choices as a human being are governed by faith and not just on personal whim or preference.

A fifth characteristic of human faith is steadfast love. Faith without steadfast love is absent; however, faith with steadfast love is eternal.

Love here is not merely the power of emotions but an act of the will. Love means that I will that others will abide in goodness for themselves, their families, and their endeavors. Steadfast love supersedes amorist feelings or loving behavior. It is helping others make life-giving choices.

A good example of understanding how faith translates into steadfast love can be seen in the character of Mrs. Cratchit. She, although a minor character in *A Christmas Carol*, exemplifies her steadfast love toward her family who are impoverished financially but rich in goodness. Her maternal optimism in the face of adversity bores out her conviction that good can come out of less rather than more despite her family's poverty-stricken condition. This belief of hers is anchored in her steadfast love. The Cratchits' poverty-stricken situation is viewed as a blessing, not a curse.

We first meet Mrs. Cratchit in the part of the story where Scrooge is traveling with the Ghost of Christmas Present. In some adaptations of the novella, she has been identified as Emily. Although Mrs. Cratchit may appear as a simple, naive, and guileless woman, she is a headstrong, disciplined, and assertive wife and mother. This is evident of her criticism of her husband's employer, Mr. Scrooge, when her husband, Bob, remarked in making a family toast, "I'll give you, Mr. Scrooge, the Founder of the Feast!" To which Mrs. Cratchit cried reddeningly, "The Founder of the Feast, indeed. I wish I had him here. I'd give him a piece of my mind to feast upon, and

I hope he'd have a good appetite for it. It should be Christmas-day, I am sure on which one drinks the health of such an odious, stingy, hard unfeeling man as Mr. Scrooge. You know he is, Robert! Nobody knows it better than you do, poor fellow!" To which Bob responds mildly, "My dear! Christmas-day." Mrs. Cratchit continues with her rant, 'I'll drink his health for your sake and the Day's, not for his. Long life to him! A merry Christmas and a happy New Year! He'll be very merry and very happy; I have no doubt!"

We read Mrs. Cratchit is dressed out in a poorly twice-turned gown braved in ribbons that are cheap, which means she is wearing a dress that has been made over twice, indicating she cannot afford to buy new clothes. We begin to understand that Mrs. Cratchit is used to having scanty, meaning she shows "great delight" at the fact that there is "one small atom of bone" remaining of their Christmas goose at the end of their feast. Mrs. Cratchit rejoices that they hadn't eaten it all at last, yet everyone had enough.[28]

It is not that the Cratchits were very stingy and frugal, but they were poverty-stricken. Dickens accentuates this in contrast to Scrooge's limitless appetite for more comfort and wealth. Again, this theme is revisited and symbolized by how the family reacts to Mrs. Cratchit's Christmas pudding. Although she brings the pudding to the table with much pomp and circumstance where everyone in the family admires it, we discover the small size of the pudding for so large a family, like many other aspects of their Christmas celebration are heightened by their gratitude and optimism. This presentation of the Christmas pudding to the table is further validated by her husband, who remarks as the text reads,

> "Oh, a wonderful pudding!" Bob Cratchit said, and calmly too, that he regarded it as the greatest success achieved by Mrs. Cratchit since their marriage.
>
> Mrs. Cratchit said that, now the weight was off her mind, she would confess she had her doubts about the quantity of flour. Everybody

had something to say about it, but nobody said or thought it was at all a small pudding for a large family. It would have been flat heresy to do so. Any Cratchit would have blushed to hint at such a thing. (Stave 3—"The Second of the Three Spirits")

Their love for one another is paramount and steadfast. The pudding stands as a symbol of how and what they share together. Mrs. Cratchit raised her six children well in this regard, which is validated by her husband Bob's humble and generous spirit. Hence the expression "The proof is in the pudding" describes the family's gratitude for whatever they receive as blessing. This is indeed steadfast love they shared. This indeed is a family of faith. This gift of steadfast love was perpetuated by Mrs. Cratchit's exaggerated but authentic optimism.

In the biblical Hebrew scriptures, the word *hesed* defines what faith is as lived by the Cratchits. It was a term that described the love relationship between their God and the people of Israel.

Loosely translated in English, it means "steadfast love" or "faithful love."

Its meaning is more visceral than these English translations. This love was understood in the context of a covenant that you make with another person. The concept of covenant was not only legally binding in Jewish tradition but one made "in blood." This meant one gave oneself fully and completely without reservation to another. It connoted a superlative commitment made by one to another where life is shared in loving-kindness. The sacred concept *hesed* appears in the Torah more than 190 times, denoting true devotion expressing one's premier relationship. It is through this loving-kindness to others that one ultimately finds oneself.

*Faith as Divine Reality*

Faith in the Divine tears down the barrier between time and eternity.

> It is not enough to simply lay out the plans of our lives, as thoughtful as they may be, to ensure our plans are as solid, we are called to share our plans with the master builder and listen for a response. We stay in dialogue with the builder to make adjustments that are needed, even to start again if necessary. Building a full and sturdy life, exposed as we are to all kinds of elements, demands a strong foundation.[29]

That is exactly what faith in the Divine requires and demands—a relationship beyond time and ultimately an orientation to the master builder whom we have identified as God.

As we discussed, the enemy of faith is fear. So too this is evident with faith in the Divine. For faith in the Divine, the major premise is that life has the mission of preparing us for death despite fear. It sounds a bit morbid, but one who lives defying fear with faith can resolve this morbidity. This is the power of faith in the Divine. In discussing how faith in the Divine is real, grounded in reality, and not merely virtual or fantasy, it would be well to be acquainted with the story of a Frenchwoman named Madeleine Delbrêl.[30] Her life brought the reality of faith to another level, some would say a supernatural one.

Madeleine Delbrêl, born in 1904 in Mussidan, located in the southwestern part of France, was the child of nonreligious parents and took fancy in becoming an atheist by the time she was fifteen years old. She lived a rather isolated life since she couldn't make friends because her family was constantly moving from place to place during her childhood. She inherited her father's talent of writing. As a young adult, she experienced many significant and heart-wrenching disappointments, which dampened her enthusiasm about life. These disappointments culminated with her fiancé suddenly leaving her to join the Dominican Order. Her father going blind and her parents becoming estranged to each other did not encourage her to have a positive worldview. She was devastated and perceived life to be absurd living, a life devoid of middle-class values. Despite these obstacles, she continued with her writings and illustrating poetry, studying philosophy and art at the Sorbonne in Paris. Her rebellious spirit resulted in her cutting her hair short, fashioning her own clothes, and hosting parties with intellectuals at the Sorbonne. Her atheistic outlook in life was highlighted at the age of seventeen when she wrote a tract entitled "God Is Dead—Long Live Death," which expressed her manifesto that death is the only certainty in life.

At the age of twenty-four, she writes that she found God through her Christian friends, who exhibited that life didn't appear absurd to them since they engaged in all the pleasurable leisure activities she did and enjoyed life to the full. Suddenly, in her perception, God's existence did not seem as completely impossible anymore, and so she began her conversion to Christianity by reading the works of Teresa of Ávila, which inspired her to pray to God as if God was someone to love like any other person. Madeleine through her newly found spirituality in prayer led her to the belief that God found her. Although she briefly considered joining the Carmelite Order, which was the religious community that Teresa of Ávila belonged, she felt she could as easily go into the world and help women in France to achieve their goals by obtaining a degree in social studies in Ivry, France. She subsequently was employed by the city government of Ivry where she assisted the youth, the poor, and the women with their social needs simply caring, consoling, and advocating for people in need. This she continued to do throughout World War II. Her obsession with death now took on a different dimension where she now viewed herself as a missionary working closely with the urban working class and founded a house of hospitality in response to the needs of the poor. Madeleine's philosophy of life changed from being directed by her obsession with death to seeing death as a transition from human life to eternal life. She has been referred to as the "French Dorothy Day."[31]

A taste of the fruits of her conversion to Christianity and abandonment of her pessimistic thought process about death as the finality of one's existence is seen in her writings viewing death as transition into the eternal, not merely the end of life:

> Life has the job of preparing us for death; and it knows its job well. We only have to listen to life, watch it well, and follow it. It explains death to us by little or in one fell swoop, depending on the day. Sometimes without doing any harm at all, all other times tearing us apart with grief. Sometimes by underlining the small deaths that we endure each day, at others by laying out in death those whom we love more than our own selves.
>
> We learn about death as we comb our hair in the morning and find that our hair is getting

thin; when the tooth that has been aching for a long while leaves us.

When our skin wrinkles at the corner of our eyes; when we can say as we tell some trifling story: "Two years ago, twenty or thirty years ago." When each year they come with flowers to wish us a happy birthday; flowers which are slightly suggestive of the cemetery and—we ourselves remain and that celebrate one less year to go.

We learn about death at each reunion with those who preserve our childhood and among whom we remain children, or when our memory starts to slip away from us and our mobility is not what it was, these parts of our nature death invade early. We learn about death each time we are torn definitively from our loved ones. For even though our faith, our hope of reunion, and even our love for them affirms our joy—the joy of knowing that they have gone home—we ourselves remain, with our blood protesting and our flesh torn and hurt.

Life is our teacher when it comes to death—we who know we have experienced human repentance. By becoming familiar with death, we learn to become familiar with life. It's like making a conversion to the dimension of the eternal, as when we look at the negatives of a film to get the picture. We have to open the eye of faith in those circumstances where our own eyes fail us. When we look at our garden, we are not stunned to see the yellowing of a blade of grass, so let's be sufficiently interested in eternity so that all that we love may already be transferred into the calm of eternity. In this way we will learn to die to death and so live authentically. forever.[32]

What is faith in the Divine then? Is this something concocted by religion? Is it a human attempt to deal with the finality of death?

Is the belief in the afterlife a psychological projection of self to make sense of the struggles and pains of our existence?

I think without even turning to any religious tradition for an answer, the point of departure for an answer lies in the self itself. Carl Jung, prolific and legendary psychiatrist, in ascertaining how the self defines our personality and makes choices with the understanding that each individual is called to attain one's own wholeness, may give us some insight.[33] Wholeness lies in the developing dialogue between the self (Jung would later refer to it as the "God image" and one's ego [center of conscious willing and striving]).[34]

I am not implying that the Divine is a sheer psychological projection of the self couched in religious beliefs to deal with the travails of life such as human suffering, pain, and death in order to find meaning in existence. Rather, I think that the Divine is a reality unto itself beyond our finitude, which ultimately seeks communion with humanity.

In a sense, the reality of the Divine becomes a calling for humanity to reach its full realization of goodness, truth, and love. The self for Jung was considered a divine principle—"the God image" within each human psyche, which made the soul's individuation possible. Jung understood God's call to each person as a call to the realization of his or her own wholeness for the purpose of attaining individuation and self-autonomy. Individuation is a fundamental developmental process to achieve consciousness of self.

In a letter written a few years before his death, Jung spoke about his use of the term *God* with respect to his experience of an autonomous agent in the psyche.[35] He spoke about his use of the term *God* in his letters to reflect upon his personal experience of "the Other" throughout his life as realized in dreams, visions, and voices and came to the conclusion that God was no "illusion."[36] Jung's deepest convictions found expression as evidenced by an inscription carved over the doorway of his house in Küsnacht near Zurich in Switzerland, which read in Latin, "Vocatus atque non vocatus Deus aderit," translated

"Called and not called, God will be there." Jung said he put this inscription there to remind his patients and himself that the fear of the Lord is the beginning of wisdom. We do not know if Jung was a religious person or not; however, his understanding of the human psyche as having a "calling" testifies to a spiritual dimension present in the human mind. This denotes at best he was a spiritual person.

He attested that the materials in the depth of the psyche cannot be reduced simply to causes in the personal history of each individual, but each psyche moves toward the recognition of the role of symbols and myth in the life of the individual to seek the Divine. Jung considered God "one of the soul's deepest and closest intimacies."[37]

The archetypes of the collective unconscious of the mind for which Jung's theory of the self is best known for is where relationship with the Divine is possible.[38] The goal in life as far as Jung was concerned is to discover one's myth of meaning in one's life. The myth is the story we find that tells us who we are, which must include some explanation of the meaning of human existence in the cosmos. In other words, we need to ask ourselves when we receive "the calling," what is the meaning of our human existence in the realm of the cosmos?

This "calling" is identified by Jung as inner leadings—that is, to respond yes to someone or something that makes one certain that existence is meaningful, and therefore, my life in self-surrender has a goal. We do not dictate what this leading is. The ego, Jung contends, must surrender to this "lead," for we do not create "God." We chose him.[39] This psychological perspective needs as its foundation one basic theological tenet, and that is that faith in the Divine involves mystery.

Faith in the Divine whether we attribute the Divine to be God or "one's higher power" or "the Almighty" or the "creator" or the "ultimate life source" or the "uncaused cause" or the "ultimate consciousness" has to do with two powerful dynamics. These two dynamics are transcendence and immanence. Both dynamics involve mystery and are complementary attributes of a higher life intelligence.

Transcendence refers to a higher intelligence, which is a completely different kind of substance from and completely independent of the material universe, beyond all known physical laws. Transcendence in the religious experience of faith is a state of being that has superseded the limitations of physical experience. Transcendence can be attributed to a Divine being not only by its omnipresence but also by its limitless knowledge. A being that transcends is beyond the grasp of our human psyche. It's being, presence, and knowledge transcend all and are infinite, e.g., Judaism's understanding of God in the Torah.

Immanence refers to a higher intelligence that is inherent, lives within, and sustains all beings as its effective cause. Immanence is the balancing concept of transcendence. Many times, immanence incorrectly gets equivocated with pantheism. It gets erroneously associated with the New Age or *Star Wars*-esque understanding of the "force." The distinctive difference is that pantheism claims an impersonal power or force, which not only inhibits or sustains everything but ultimately is everything. On the other hand, immanence, when applied to a living being, is distinguishable from all matter that sustains all but is not everything, nor is everything somehow a piece or part of the immanence of a higher being. Immanence means a superior being is omnipresent to all living beings and to all matter but not "in" all things. Immanence is defined as a higher being fully present in the physical world and completely accessible to it.

Although transcendence and immanence appear to be opposites, the two are not necessarily mutually exclusive but complementary. They are two sides of the same coin. The "coin" being a higher living intelligence that has the capacity to know and to love and possesses both dynamics at the same time. We have already established what the essence of being human is—believing and living in relationship with another human being with the capacity to know and love, to be known and be loved.

The essence of this relationship becomes the point of departure in seeking how faith can transition one from the natural journey in this life to the divine realm. Faith as we have come to understand is a stance or totally committed lifestyle akin to what it means to be unconditionally and totally human. To be totally and unconditionally human is to be divine. This doesn't mean perfection but a total and unconditional self-giving. Being human is not a blemish or imperfection of the Divine, but when totally actualized, it is the "image of the Divine." Take, for example, the Christian theology of Jesus Christ as the manifestation of "God became man [human] so that man [humanity] might become God."[40]

This is how a conversation can begin by discussing how faith as human reality can transition into a continuum of life into the unknown endless realm of the Divine. The human faith experience with the finality of death is open-ended and allows for the possibility of life continuing into the beyond.

For the purpose of our discussion, we will identify the beyond as the infinitude of all realities. Upon the transformation of life with death, one no longer sees reality through the "eyes of faith" but through the prism of "seeing in plain sight" what is eternal.

Is divine existence a blueprint or template of what it means to be unconditionally and totally human? If so, then it follows that the Divine is the ultimate reality of what it means to be unconditionally human.

To be totally and unconditionally human necessitates a personal relationship of knowing and being known, to love and being loved. Again, this is the essence of being human. If we speak of the Divine in terms of relationship, then it is not out of the question to expect that what we experience in this relationship is comparable to human relationships. Relationships of humans with humans follow a continuum of life until death and then, hereafter, transforms to a relationship of humans with fellow humans in a communion of divine life, which is perfected in unconditional and steadfast love.

Traditionally, religion has to call this continuum of eternal life heaven. Faith is that conduit that allows one to traverse from the pilgrimage of believing in everyday human encounters into the climax of experiencing full communion with the Divine. We have come to identify the Divine to be God. Love becomes that "connective" reality and fabric of that communion brought to fruition by faith. Faith becomes those inner leadings (in Jung's words) to eternal life. Faith in the Divine necessitates a "wholeness of self" that is a full and clear consciousness of self upon encountering the source of all life—God. For it is, as Carl Jung describes divine presence in the self, "called and not called, God will be there."

All this talk of transcendence and immanence in describing the realm of the Divine leads us to understanding faith in the Divine as mystery. God is mystery. The realm of the Divine—heaven is likewise mystery. Without mystery, there is no faith in the Divine since faith in the Divine is mystery itself. We encounter eternal mystery when we encounter death and thus enter the divine realm. The divine realm refers to the infinitude of being, which is celestial and a totally spiritual reality. It is not a place in time but a different stratum of existence beyond time.

Mystery is a complex and fascinating reality that has multiple meanings. It can mean anything from the mundane reality of experiencing suspense in reading a novel, enjoying a play, or viewing a movie dealing with a puzzling crime or murder to the sublimity of a religious experience. Mystery involves the intangible, the noncorporeal, the incorruptible, the spiritual, and the infinite. Mystery is identified with realities of the beyond, the unexplainable, realities outside of space and linear time, and is the ultimate unknown.

Mystery means we can never have the final word about the Divine; there is always more to discover, there is always more to share, and there is always more to experience. In that sense, the mystery of the Divine invites us never to abandon the endless task of growing as humans but to understand the wisdom that underlies our world.

It challenges us never to abandon faith, which power brings us to the precipice of eternity. It humbles us. It makes us appreciative of humility and how precious our lives are. Our journey beyond this life through faith brings us to the One who is the ground of existence—the One we have come to identify as God. Our journey toward God and toward one another in this existence is made along the same road. That road is faith.

It is the road of faith that comes to a climax when it comes to its final destination—God, which is life eternal. Faith allows us to grow and leap into the odyssey of eternity where its final destination is communion with all those who share full life in the Divine. This Supreme Being or Divine intelligence is personal, intimate, and immanent because this divine presence yearns for a relationship with humanity. Only a personal, intimate, and living reality capable of knowing and loving can engage in a relationship. This is the "calling" referred to by Jung in discussing the self as "the God image" on the way to full self-autonomy and liberation. This God is one, an undivided communion and a relational mystery since the created love emitted is always in terms of a relationship. Faith finds its completion and final resting place in the divine presence where we no longer see through "the eyes of faith" but experience the fullness of life in an unapproachable light in plain sight.

In Christian theology, for example, the fullness of divine presence is called the beatific vision, which is the ultimate direct self-communication of God with each individual being. The reality of mystery comes into play by the fact that ready or not, the most ultimate and final human event that will be experienced by all is death. Paradoxically, faith in the Divine means we must experience death to enjoy life eternal. Faith in the Divine means I take the ultimate risk accepting death as part of being human so that I can transition into the fullness of life and love. Faith beckons the self to transcend upon death to its ultimate eternal continuum of life. This was the message of Madeleine Delbrêl concerning how life prepares us to encounter death so that we can move on without fear. This is what communion with the Divine does. It allows human beings not only to share in divinity but also to be divine. This we have come to identify as the state of being we call heaven. Heaven is not a place but a state of being in communion with the Divine and with all those formerly human beings now celestial in the realm of eternity. This is what faith in the Divine mystery means. It is not a religion but a life—an eternal life.

The life of a human being is destined from a contingent existence to the awesome experience of eternal bliss, light, and love. The Divine is the true home and ultimate calling of humanity, which has laboriously journeyed the road of faith. Faith in the Divine demands that I be open and vulnerable to the experience of death so that I can transition into divine life. This is only true when one is imbued with faith. This implies that when faith becomes part of one's self as free gift and choice, there is a power or "vibrant life presence" in that human being operative during the earthly sojourn that make it not only spiritual but also attracted to and attracted by the divine realm. Traditionally, this is defined as one's soul or spirit.

The spirit is not a "life force" but a real, personal, and true presence begotten from relationship. The soul or spirit are not philosophical platonic forms but a life presence finding completion in a communion of relationship. Where there is no relationship, there is no need for faith. If there is no faith, relationship with the Divine is nonexistent. The state of existence that defines this communion or celestial relationship with the Divine and with other beings who are now part of the divine realm is called heaven. Human love, the fruit of faith in the Divine, is the fire and soul of one's being in the earthly sojourn, which brings one to full realization of the Divine.

Just as we identified five characteristics of faith as human reality, analogously, faith in the Divine is characterized by three dynamic realities. These realities are symbolized by three dimensions.

The dimensions are *eternal light, eternal voice,* and *eternal life.*

Eternal *light,* eternal *voice,* and eternal *life* are the living dimensions of faith in the Divine. Eternal light, eternal voice, and eternal life permeate human existence so as to attract one to a continuum of life upon death. It is this celestial light, piercing voice, and immortal life of the Divine that faith employs to enlighten, speak, and energize the human heart. Faith makes us like earthen vessels, fragile but unbreakable, holding us to and directing us on a course that soars into the beyond where everything is experienced in an unapproachable light, heard as a melodious voice, and rests ultimately in eternal bliss.

John Henry Newman, a prominent English clergyman, theologian, and poet, describes the celestial light of faith, which enlightens human reason in the following way:[41]

> Lead kindly Light, amidst th' encircling gloom
> Lead thou me on!
> The night is dark, and I am far from home.
> Lead thou me on!
> Keep thou, my feet; I do not ask to see
> the distant scene; one step enough for me
> I was not ever thus, nor prayed that thou
> Shouldst lead me on;
> I love to choose and see my path; but now
> Lead thou me on!
> I loved the garish day, and, spite of fears,
> Pride ruled my will: remember not past years!
> So long thy power hath blessed me, sure it still
> Will lead me on.
> O'er moor and fen, o'er crag and torrent, till
> the night is gone.
> And with the morn those angel faces smile
> Which I have loved long since, and lost a while!

Natural light helps us and others to see what already exists in our own person, families, neighborhood, place of employment, etc. Without light, we enter a dark room and stumble over hidden objects, fall, and hurt ourselves and others. With light, we recognize chairs, tables, doors, and walls of the room. We can sit down and rest, we can eat at the table, we can see the lovely photos and the pictures on the wall, and we can walk to other parts of the home. Light, therefore, brings harmony, good relationships, enrichment, and color into our lives. Light also induces growth. Plants and flowers seek light. Light illumines our world with warmth, love, happiness, and new life.

As with the light of faith, the radiance of light activates enlightenment and inspiration. It becomes a catalyst for action. When we experience light, we can assess the darkness in retrospect. It helps to shed focus on the choices we need to make as we move about in our daily lives.

The light always involves making realities present so that we can make good choices. It is here that we can decipher by light's radiance what actions led us into darkness and unhealthy behaviors morally, psychologically, and socially. It is the same light that radiates us to reform, change, or convert to goodness and leave the darkness by abandoning unhealthy and self-centered behaviors.

The eternal light born of faith is that beacon that governs our common sense and grounds us in reality to make virtuous choices. These choices not only embellish human life but also direct us to eternal life. The eternal light is "the good eye" that is filled with inspiration and able to see goodness and righteousness in the actions and hearts of others. Rather than be annoyed by the faults, idiosyncrasies, and shortcomings of others, we need to appreciate the good side of people's character. This is what the light of faith does. It demands that we commend people for their virtues, not condemn them for vices, and not imitate the annoying traits of people's self-bragging and boasting. But if we brag, let it be for our suffering, diligence, and efforts to profess our faith despite our human frailties and failures.

The same may be true of the "eternal voice." It is not an auditory hallucination, illusion, or "direct voice" from God but again an "internal lead" (in Jung's words when he speaks of the unconscious) to follow one's own visceral inner calling beyond one's emotional gut or instinct. The eternal voice lies in the recesses of the human heart—e.g., the experience of falling in love. Or it could be one made in silence and solitude—e.g., a conversion to a specific religious lifestyle or profession of service. This "voice" is a calling and an attraction for one to give heed and "stop in one's tracks" and listen and subsequently follow.

Many have identified this "inner voice" as a calling or vocation. The eternal voice could also be a mysterious experience, which results in a person's conversion or life reform, e.g., Saul of Tarsus, who became Paul the Apostle, whose conversion was recounted in the Christian scriptures (Acts 9). The eternal voice needs to be discerned among all the sounds and noise of our busy lives. Many times, it comes in the silence of our lives, not in a roar but in a whisper.

I like to describe the eternal voice inspired by faith by quoting one of my favorite baseball sportswriters, Thomas Verducci, who wrote a very inspirational reflection called "The Voice of God," which appeared in a 2019 edition of the *Magnificat*, a monthly Catholic magazine.

> There is a mountain out West I like to climb whenever I visit there. As I climb, I am wishing that when I get to the top, I will have that small space to myself. As much as the view and the rest, it is the silence that I seek. For up there, where the wind whispers, the birds glide without care, and the earth curves away in every direction, it is in the quiet that I can hear the voice of God... [what] caused me to reflect upon was not just the place and moment but also how we hear God... When Abraham prostrated himself, God spoke to him. There is no mention of anyone with him. Abraham, an old man, lying prone, is the very picture of giving oneself to God. Having quieted himself and his world, Abraham listens well. He does not speak. He learns of this "everlasting covenant" with God... [As compared to a gospel reading] there is much more noise. Jesus is speaking to a crowd of Jews. They are doubtful. They challenge him when he invokes Abraham and God. Their skepticism grows into intent to harm. They pick up stones to throw at Jesus, who must engineer his escape. Amid serenity, the heart and mind open easily to God; monasteries

and retreats, for instance do not have Main Street addresses. It is amid the noise of everyday life, and the influence of crowds and doubters, that it is not so easy. But the voice of God is there amid the noise just the same as amid the quiet. He calls us always, and it is upon us to listen well—mountaintop not required.

Eternal life, the third dimension of faith in the divine mystery, is an enormous reality that encompasses both eternal light (inspiration) and eternal voice (inner urgings of the heart). It too is an attraction and gravitates the center of the human being from within where faith resides. It drives us beyond our humanity and comforts of creaturehood to infinity. Faith tells us this is so. Faith doesn't prove it or document it but points that eternal life is the ultimate concern of human existence. It is the ultimate reality of communion of humanity with the divine realm, surpassing all religious experiences, philosophies of life, and relationships that we have ever encountered. There is a spark of eternal life in every human heart, but it needs to be cultivated and redirected by faith so that, at death, it can soar back to its true home.

I like to define that the life beyond us as "faith proof." I like to think of it as part of ourselves that is activated, immortalized, and soars beyond this world to seek its true home. Upon death, this human reality of faith becomes divine mystery. The mystery is more profound and beyond any expression of religion, but at the same time, it is the foundation of all religions. Obviously, I am at a loss of words to speculate about the life after death since no one has ever returned from the death to tell us what to expect (not withstanding and with all due respect to the Christian belief that Jesus Christ rose from the dead). We can only surmise what the afterlife is by using our imagination along with the beliefs and descriptions provided by many religious traditions, metaphysical philosophies, and cultures.

When we discuss the mystery of eternal life, we need to speak of the divine realm. We can define the divine realm generally as the personal "territory" and topographical expression of a deity. The root of the word *divine* is literally "godly," but the term varies depending upon what deity one is discussing. In monotheistic faiths such as Christianity, Judaism, and Islam, divinity is often used to refer to a singular God who is central to the faith and has a relationship with its adherents.

When the term takes on a definite article such as "the divinity," it is used as a proper name as compared to using the term uncapitalized and lacking the definite article used to denote "gods" seen many times in the world of mythology. For the Divine to have relevancy for humanity, it needs to encounter the human world. This is what occurs when there is a relationship between the two. There needs to be human awareness and consciousness that this encounter is happening. Divine intervention is a necessary encounter in history as viewed by the powers that accompany it. This divine intervention consists of transcendence and immanence as we have discussed. They are the dynamics that are operative in discussing eternal life. Monotheistic faiths such as Christianity, Judaism, and Islam view both of these dynamics as operative of divine providence. This acknowledges that the Divine has a profound mysterious plan always unfolding in world events. No matter how the term is used, divinity in numberless sacred texts of various religious persuasions always refers to what is beyond the human sphere, i.e., unlimited in power, endless in knowledge, immortal in existence, and the culmination of love perfected. All this is what eternal life encompasses. In short, the divine realm is the world of mystery. Without mystery, there is no faith in the Divine. Faith as divine mystery always involves faith in the divine realm, which is defined as eternal life. Faith as divine mystery means we look not to what is seen but to what is unseen, for what is seen is transitory, but what is unseen is eternal (2 Corinthians 4:18).

In summary, the three realities of faith in the Divine—eternal *light*, eternal *voice*, and eternal *life*—tell us that we are in the midst of divine mystery. In living amid divine mystery, the faith experience is consummated, hope becomes reality, life becomes everlasting, knowledge is infinite, and love is forever. Our sole human response to divine mystery can only be that we stand in awe of the depth of its reality and let it consume us. Divine mystery is not to be proven or historically documented since that is what mystery is not. It is to be held in awe, reverenced in gratitude for the immensity of its presence.

Mystery is at the heart of faith. Revelation of what or who the Divine is will not be disclosed until we become part of the divine realm where faith will no longer be needed. We will see eternity in plain sight.

One may ask then, what does this last section on faith as divine mystery have to do with the message of *A Christmas Carol*? The answer is human love. This human love gets elevated to being divine. The love of Bob Cratchit for his wife and she for him and their love together for their six children and reciprocated back to them is what Dickens's carol is about. It is the love Fred (Scrooge's nephew) has for his beloved, the love that Fan has for her husband and for Ebenezer when no one showed it toward him. It is the love old Fezziwig had for his wife and family, which included his employees, which demon-strated divine presence in the world of business. We are never so helplessly unhappy as when we lose love (Sigmund Freud).

The old expression "It is better to have loved and lost than to never have loved at all" is certainly true in the life of Ebenezer Scrooge, who learned to love in his early years despite his father's animosity toward him due to the fact that Ebenezer was born at the cost of his mother not surviving childbirth. This along with his love relationship with Belle, his longtime fiancée, was all Ebenezer knew of love until it was abruptly replaced by his new love—the lust for wealth.

What does human love look like? How is it experienced? Love is always embodied in human relationships, which demonstrate joy, altruism, peace, patience, kindness, goodness, empathy, faithfulness, gentleness, fortitude, trust, fidelity to the truth, hope in the future, meekness of heart, mercy, honesty, perseverance and persistence, self-affirmation, respect, admiration and passion for the sacredness of the human body, unity of spirit, tenderness, self-giving, forgiveness, and generosity of life. If these are the attributes of human love, what then is divine love? It is the bond of perfection. It can be capsulized in this line from the Christian scriptures: "God is love, and those who abide in love abide in God and God abides in them" (1 John 4:16). Many religious traditions, spiritual mantras, and metaphysical philosophies have similar phrases describing the immensity and depth of love.

Our participation in the cosmic process of communion with the Divine calls us to continue as human beings toward self-awareness and toward wholeness of one's consciousness with being in the world. Similar to Ebenezer Scrooge's earthly journey in life, we too struggle through the lures of the pleasures of life where all things of this world are fleeting.

It is in that world one needs to find final rest in love—humanity's redemption. Our participation in the cosmic process of communion with the Divine goes beyond therapeutic mindfulness to a full realization of who we are as human beings, how we are valued, and what our destiny is as citizens of this earth. Faith is that conduit to disclose those truths about our true worth and destiny. Faith's goal is communion with eternal life. Whether this goal is achieved through religious expression or not, it is nevertheless the power, the drive, and impetus of faith to achieve wholeness—consciousness with the divine realm. In the Christian tradition, as with many other religious traditions, the spirit of God (Holy Spirit) is identified as the vibrant divine presence within each human being that develops an attraction during its earthly sojourn to return home to the divine realm. In the Judaic tradition of the scriptures, the term *ruah*, which appears in the creation narrative of the book of Genesis, depicts the winds denoting the spirit of God who creates. The human finds its origins in "the image of God." It doesn't involve making out each human as a "God" but on the contrary realizing that within each human being lies the potential of responding to God by bringing that dynamic encounter into consciousness. This was Jung's contribution to what he meant by "wholeness of self"—to bring the encounter with the Divine into one's consciousness.

That is the faith that is behind the chain we forged in life, and as Jacob Marley says, "I made it link by link, and yard by yard; I girded it on of my own free will, and of my own free will I wore it" (stave 1—"Marley's Ghost").

# CHAPTER 2

# Self-Transformation—a Second Chance

---

Business! mankind was my business. The common
welfare was my business. Charity, mercy, forbearance
and benevolence were, all my business.

—Jacob Marley

In the opening stave, the business at hand for Scrooge as spoken by his deceased partner, Jacob Marley, was the invitation to self-reclamation or transformation or, in Marley's words, "a chance and hope of escaping my fate." The fate being that the spirit within a man should walk abroad among his fellow men and travel far and wide, and if that spirit goes not forth in life, it is condemned to do so after death. It is doomed to wander the world and witness what it cannot share but might have shared on earth.

It is the business of the life process of self-transformation and procuring second chances in life that gives *A Christmas Carol* its eminence for which Dickens, like many of us, struggle to achieve. Self-transformation was the goal not only for Dickens's characters but also for him and is also for us too.

Self-transformation always involves leaving one place or state of mind to traverse courageously to another place or state of mind. It always entails anxiety of going into the unknown from the familiar where one has been most comfortable. It always seems to involve a struggle, a resistance, and most times a conflict whether external or internal where hard work is needed for positive changes to occur. Self-transformation not only demands discipline of mind and spirit but also always entails receiving support from those we trust in making the necessary transitions. Self-transformation leaves us being most vulnerable and many times ashamed and dissatisfied how are lives have been.

The foundation and primary characteristic of transformation is faith, which we have already explored in all its dimensions in the previous chapter.

A second key ingredient of self-transformation is generosity.

Human generosity is the extension to reaching out to another with heartfelt empathy, kindness, and self-giving. We have seen this attribute in *A Christmas Carol* as portrayed by Dickens, particularly in the character of "old Fezziwig." He is described as a jovial, selfless merchant to whom Scrooge attributes his business training as a young apprentice. The Fezziwigs are portrayed as the perfect happy family. Like Mr. Fezziwig, they are larger than life with the love of music, dance, food, drink, and merrymaking. Dickens makes this family synonymous with Christmas itself, connecting them to the simple joys of warmth of friendship, the colors of one's festive attire, and the joy of family. The Fezziwig family represents what is good about life—generosity, family, fun, and joy. Dickens goes out of his way in presenting a long description in his novella of the Fezziwig Christmas gala. It shows the importance of what existed in Scrooge's young life and what he lost when he wedded wealth. Fezziwig's ball is a colorful, musical, and joyous gala that illuminates Scrooge's conscience to reconsider his wretched behavior toward his employee, Bob Cratchit.

Although Fezziwig is renowned for his Christmas parties, his generosity abounds for not only inviting his employees each year but also including the local townspeople to be part of his family's celebration. Fezziwig's abounding generosity makes Scrooge regret how poorly he has treated his own clerk, Bob Cratchit. Dickens along with Scrooge's words describes the goodness and generosity of Fezziwig as he converses with the Spirit of Christmas Past:

> [Scrooge remarks] "Why, its old Fezziwig! Bless his heart, it's Fezziwig alive again!" Old Fezziwig [as he wore his Welsh wig] laid down his pen, and looked up at the clock, which pointed to the hour of seven. He rubbed his hands, adjusted his capacious waistcoat; laughed all over himself, from his shoes to his organ of benevolence; and called out, in a comfortable, oily, rich, fat, jovial voice: 'Yo ho, there! Ebenezer! Dick!' Scrooge's former self, now grown a young man, came briskly in, accompanied by his fellow-'prentice. "Dick Wilkins, to be sure!"
>
> said Scrooge to the Ghost. "Bless me, yes. There he is. He was very much attached to me, was Dick. Poor Dick! Dear, dear!" "Yo ho, my boys!" said Fezziwig. "No more work tonight. Christmas-eve, Dick. Christmas, Ebenezer! Let's have the shutters up," cried old Fezziwig with a sharp clap of his hands, "before a man can say Jack Robinson!"… "Hilli-ho!" cried old Fezziwig skipping down from the high desk with wonderful agility. "Clear away, my lads, and let's have lots of room here!" Hilli-ho, Dick! Chirrup, Ebenezer!" Clear away! There was nothing they wouldn't have cleared away, or couldn't have cleared away, with old Fezziwig looking on… During the whole of this time [experiencing the dancing, the music of the fiddler, the enormous spread of food and great hospitality rendered to

all by the entire Fezziwig family] Scrooge had acted like a man out of his wits. His heart and soul were in the scene, and with his former self. He corroborated everything, remembered everything, enjoyed everything and underwent the strangest agitation… "A small matter" said the Ghost, "to make these silly folks so full of gratitude." "Small!" echoed Scrooge. The Spirit signed to him to listen to the two apprentices, who were pouring out their hearts in praise of Fezziwig; and, when he had done so, said: "Why! Is it not!? He [Fezziwig] has spent but a few pounds of your mortal money: three or four, perhaps. Is it so much that he deserves this praise?" To which Scrooge responded heatedly to the Ghost "It isn't that, Spirit. He [Fezziwig] has the power to render us happy or unhappy; to make our service light or burdensome; a pleasure or a toil." [Scrooge continued] "Say that his power lies in words and looks; in things so slight and insignificant that it is impossible to add and count' em up: what then? The happiness he gives is quite as great as if it cost a fortune." At which point Scrooge realized and reflected how poorly in contrast he treats his employee—Bob Cratchit—as Scrooge said—"I should like to be able to say a word or two to my clerk just now. That's all." (Stave 2—"The First of the Three Spirits")

Second to faith, generosity is the second pillar of self-transformation. Generosity is beyond being kind to another. It exceeds beyond giving one's due out of respect. Its nature is to be boundless without reservation. Generosity is heeding the call of faith with action. Generosity is not just being well-intentioned but also being authentic in our actions. After one is imbued with faith, the action of generosity is the losing of self in the other while maintaining one's integrity. It is the gift that expects no reward or recognition in return. Faith without generosity is hallow; in fact, it is no faith at all. Generosity without faith is likened to deluding oneself by admiring one's own face in a mirror and seeing oneself for what one is, then going off and promptly forgetting how one looks like (James 1:23–25). The Fezziwigs portray the human attribute of generosity perfectly.

Thirdly, another pillar of self-transformation is humility. Humility is the acceptance of oneself without guile or pretense. Unfortunately, in our world, humility gets a raw deal by being translated as being weak, fragile, and gullible. Humility is one's acceptance about the truth.

We hear often these days the expression, "I need to speak my truth."

I understand that this expression is in context of one's freedom to personally express oneself and no one can think, feel, or act for another. My truth is the only truth of a person if I am telling *the truth*. Similar to belief, just because I believe in something doesn't make it true, so too just because I speak my truth doesn't make a reality true.

Affirmations such as these run the risk of resulting in stupidity, which, as Coach Bill Parcells, former NFL world champion coach of the New York Giants in 1987, is quoted in saying, "Never underestimate stupidity. It always shows up." Or in the words of Forrest Gump as played by Tom Hanks in the movie *Forrest Gump*, "Stupid is what stupid does." Good behavior needs to be accountable to reality. Many times, the expression "my truth" becomes a pretentious substitute for "nonnegotiable personal opinion." It becomes a convenient phrase similar to many of the phrases of the "politically correct" generation to avoid arguments because people can contradict your opinion but not your "truth."

Often the expression "my truth" is often used when seeking to justify a controversial personal stance or action because people are not permitted to argue with "your truth." The expression "my truth" doesn't imply that people are not telling the truth but that they are steadfast in their conviction based upon their thoughts, feelings, and experiences, but my truth remains my truth—that is, my opinion, not necessarily gospel truth. Unfortunately, the term *opinion* has lost much of its luster and power these days possibly because, unfortunately, people have readily and arbitrarily disrespected and dismissed others' opinions.

So hence is born the phrase "my truth," apparently a stronger vocal affirmation, which stands up to the test of rejection or opposition. Opinion is solely an opinion; everyone has one. My truth basically redounds in being true to oneself. Humility is based upon not only my truth or your truth but also how honest I am with myself in being accountable with reality. Reality is a major player of this equation in determining this accountability whether one sees it as my truth or your truth. Without the truth, humility is futile. Without humility, the truth cannot be found.

The character who exhibits the human attribute of humility *par excellence* is Bob Cratchit. He is the definition of what it means to be humble and stand in the light of truth in dealing with the realities of life. He may at times appear as being a wimp. A wimp Bob Cratchit is not, but an authentic, transparent, honest, and humble person he certainly is. He checks all the boxes as being a person with faith, generosity, humility, and integrity. Unlike Scrooge, he is a finished product of self-transformation when the tale begins. Bob Cratchit is not perfect but does exemplify all that is good, virtuous, and true about humanity. Much of who Bob Cratchit is as described by Dickens eloquently is a prime example of the virtues of Christmas such as humility, self-giving, and forgiveness. Bob's virtue becomes the antidote of Scrooge's greed, which in turn becomes redemptive.

Bob is a symbol of forgiveness, which is the product of being humble. This is clearly seen when at the Christmas family celebration, he toasts Scrooge despite the horrible work conditions he needs to endure, which Scrooge ignores. Even toward the end of the tale in the face of Scrooge's eventual remorse, Bob is open and accepting that Scrooge has some good in him rather than be bitter or resentful of Scrooge's past offenses toward him. Bob is the linchpin of hope for his poor family who are rich in love for one another. Scrooge taunts Bob for wanting the day off to celebrate Christmas Day with his family. Bob represents the spirit of humility for his family to celebrate with gratitude what they have instead of being bitter for what they do not have. Bob demonstrates fortitude and bravery with cheerfulness in the face of grief as foretold by the Spirit of Christmas Present concerning the impending death of Tiny Tim, which would leave a huge gap in the Cratchit household.

Again, Bob inspires hope for his family by his humility to accept the kindness extended to him by Fred, Scrooge's nephew who offers solace, condolences, and help to assist his family due to the loss of Tiny Tim as predetermined by the vision of Christmas Yet to Come. All these descriptions Dickens attributes to Bob Cratchit to demonstrate that he is truly a humble and altruistic human being.

A fourth aspect of self-transformation is transparency and honesty.

We live in a world where it is very difficult for people to live the truth that makes denial and hypocrisy pervasive behaviors in relationships.

I think I can attribute this golden virtue of transparency to Scrooge's younger sister and Fred's mother, Fan. Although she is a minor character in the tale, her brief appearance in the story is worth noting and very powerful. Other than his fiancée, Belle, Scrooge loved Fan dearly. Fan is Scrooge's "foxhole rescuer" in dealing with their father, who literally disowned Scrooge when he was a child and never forgave him, blaming him for his mother's death while giving Ebenezer life at birth. Fan not only visits Ebenezer while attending boarding school but also is instrumental to what appears reconciling Ebenezer with their father, allowing him to return home from school one Christmas.

Fan is definitely an honest and amicable young woman who implicitly and probably left a smudge of kindness in her brother's heart even throughout his self-centered years of greed. Maybe that was the residual goodness that only Bob Cratchit saw in his miserable, wretched, and ungrateful employer during his trying and laborious days of being Scrooge's clerk in the coldness of the counting house. It is interesting and ironic to note that the reason for Scrooge's alienated relationship with his nephew Fred was exactly the same reason Scrooge's father became estranged to him. Both Scrooge's mother and Fan died giving birth to Ebenezer and Fred, respectively. Both were blamed by Ebenezer's father and Ebenezer himself, respectively.

Fan is deceased at the time of the story, but in the vision of the Ghost of Christmas Past, she comes to visit Scrooge in a deserted schoolhouse when he was a child and brings him happy news that she is taking him home:

He [Scrooge] was not reading now, but walking up and down despairingly. Scrooge looked at the Ghost, and, with a mournful shaking of his head, glanced anxiously toward the door. It opened; and a little girl, much younger than the boy, came darting in, and, putting her arms around his neck, and often kissing him, addressed him as her "dear, dear brother."

"I have come to bring you home, dear brother!" said the child, clapping her tiny hands, and bending down to laugh. "To bring you home, home, home!"

"Home, little Fan?" returned the boy. "Yes!" said the child, brimful of glee. "Home for good and all. Home forever and ever. Father is so much kinder than he used to be, that home's like Heaven! He spoke so gently to me one dear night when I was going to bed, that I was not afraid to ask him once more if you might come home; and he said Yes, you should; and sent me in a coach to bring you. And you're to be a man! "said the child, opening her eyes; "and are never to come back here; but first we're to be together all Christmas long, and have the merriest time in all the world." "You are quite a woman, little Fan!" exclaimed the boy. She clapped her hands and laughed, and tried to touch his head; but, being too little, laughed again, and stood on tiptoe to embrace him. Then she began to drag him, in her childish eagerness, towards the door; and he, nothing loath to go, accompanied her... "Always a delicate creature, whom a breath might have withered," said the Ghost." "But she had a large heart!" "So, she had, cried Scrooge. "You're right. I will not gainsay it, Spirit. God forbid!" "She died a woman," said the Ghost, "and had, as I think children." "One child," Scrooge returned. "True," said the Ghost. "Your nephew!" Scrooge

> seemed uneasy in his mind; and answered briefly,
> "Yes". (Stave 2—"The First of the Three Spirits")

Fan is an important character in Scrooge's past, for she represents the best of youth, innocence, and goodness and makes Scrooge's childhood gleam compared to his cold, dark present as he recalls her life with the Ghost of Christmas Past. Fan shows that Scrooge has experienced both neglect and goodness in his young life, both cruelty and generosity.

Her authenticity and transparency are a measure for Scrooge to either follow goodness and generosity in his adult life or misery and self-indulgence of his lust for wealth.

The fifth characteristic of self-transformation is conversion. It is the work of self-reformation, which means this involves hard work. Traditionally, conversion is defined as a change of heart or attitude affecting one's behavior. It is a life transition from what is distained, i.e., evil to what is good, i.e., what is healthy to what is positive. It can even be a transition from what is good to what is better. However, in all cases, it is a major transition in one's existence, which involves full determination work and full consciousness. The Greek term for conversion is *metanoia*, meaning a radical turning away from something to something else. This radical change first begins as a thought, then a willingness to move in the direction to what is good. This disposition reaches its actualization in behavior, that which is altruistic, empathetic, and compassionate. Conversion means that I am always in tune with myself while remaining in dialogue with others, meaning how will my behavior affect others? Although conversion is inner-directed, it always is in context of being other-directed, that is, how do I make changes as it relates to others? If conversion's goal is exclusively inner-directed, it becomes a glass menagerie of taking pride on working on myself. Conversion is only meaningful and real if what changes I make of myself gets translated into my behavior. It needs to be other-directed for self-transformation to take hold. The uniqueness of the process of conversion is that unless I make changes with myself first, I cannot improve my relationship with others. So inner transformation is the first step and point of departure of conversion.

The sixth and final characteristic of self-transformation, which is the most important, is the courage to be *as* Oneself. The courage to be as Oneself is the power of self-affirmation. It is the power of the individual to have the freedom to choose the good despite all distractions of life, which challenges one to stray from the truth. Self-affirmation is the self-determination to maximize all our human potential and talents to bring about good in this world. This is what it means to be fully human.

Self-transformation is the fruit of *believing in another human being for change to occur.* It is the result of self-reformation, which is the "nuts and bolts" of correcting our shortcomings and increasing our accountability to others. Self-transformation can only happen with self-determination as one's drive and doesn't happen in isolation but always in concert with the support of others. Transformation is not exclusively self-induced but always in concert with relationships with others.

This is clearly evident in the transforming character of Ebenezer Scrooge in the course of the Christmas tale. He doesn't become a believer in the goodness of people in isolation or solely on his own but with the help of three spirits, which symbolize his stages of his self-reclamation. Scrooge is able to reclaim himself as a human being because others have been involved in his life and concerned for his welfare, beginning with the least one would expect, Jacob Marley.

This was also true of its author, Charles Dickens, who learned that only by self-determination and self-affirmation was he able to raise his family of origin out of poverty to a working-class socioeconomic status. He was able to make decisions in his career as a prominent author not be bullied and cowed by dishonest, money-hungry publishers to circulate his works and sought his own resources to highlight the social ills of his day. Similar to Scrooge, all of us pass through life in developmental stages emotionally, cognitively, and spiritually so as to become more knowledgeable, productive, and loving individuals. These stages of human development cover our past, present, and future. This is symbolically represented in the Christmases past, present, and to come in Scrooge's life. All these stages of one's life are telling not only by the events that have occurred in these stages but also how relationships developed or not developed that shape one's character over a lifetime. Relationship fuels self-transformation, self-affirmation, and self-determination. It was true of Charles Dickens's life, and it is true of our own as symbolized in the life of Ebenezer Scrooge. Granted, we may not be miserable and wretched misers like Scrooge, but all of us at times are tainted by the ills of just being human.

Self-transformation is a necessary life process to become a wholesome and well-adjusted moral human being. This process as such will be closely explored in terms of discussing the parables of Scrooge's dreams, which will be the subject in chapter 4.

Self-transformation as the courage to be *as* Oneself—an authentic, empathetic, and loving human being entails taking one's responsibility in actualizing one's strengths whatever they may be and owning up to one's limitations. It is to be a self-gift giver to others. The sin or evil of not having the courage to be *as* Oneself is a lack of being or lack of existence itself. When we forfeit the *courage to be* as human beings, we give into and surrender to nonexistence. We give into the experience of nothingness, which is not only a loss of oneself but also total despair. This is not only the sin against faith but the negation of everything human. The courage to be is finding oneself by being connected to others. This is the goal of self-transformation.

A self-giver has the capacity of using one's personal talents not only for one's benefit but also for others. It is the balancing and harmony created by self-affirmation and participating in the world that allows for self-reformation. The English poet John Donne in one of his series of essays, "Meditation 17" (1623), writes "that no man is an island." He argued for the interconnectedness of all people. As human beings, it is inherent in our nature to be in a relationship with other human beings.

It is this connectiveness of people that contributes to the faith, hope, and life of humanity. It is this interconnectedness that avoids us from experiencing nothingness, which we have defined as surrendering to total despair. This interconnectedness we have identified as relationship that is instrumental in the process of self-transformation. This was accentuated as Dunne faced death being extremely ill, for we recall this popular excerpt taken from his meditation on death:

> No man is an island,
> entire of itself;
> every man is a piece of the continent,
> a part of the main.
> If a clod he washed away by the sea,
> Europe is the less,
> as well as if a promontory were,
> as well as if a manor of thy friend's
> or of thine own were.
> Any man's death diminishes me,
> because I am involved in mankind,
> and therefore never send to know for whom the bells tolls;
> it tolls for thee.

This self-affirmation is the courage to be. This is highlighted in Paul Tillich's work synonymously entitled *The Courage to Be* (1952).[42]

Tillich as philosopher and theologian argues that self-affirmation is necessary to maintain one's existence in struggling with any dangerous or painful situation in life. The situation could be physical or mental illness, i.e., anxiety, loneliness, alienation of self, self-estrangement, and ultimately the reality of death. This self-affirmation can take the form of physical courage in dealing with a physical challenge or a medical condition where mental stamina is needed for healing or the moral courage to stand up and do the right thing in a given situation.

Tillich identifies anxiety as the primary modern psychological epidemic resulting from a loss of meaning in life. Tillich identifies courage as the antidote to this modern-day spiritual epidemic challenging one not to succumb to despair in finding meaning in life.

Seeking self-affirmation is the courage to stand up and call out those elements that negate human empowerment. It is this challenge and ethical act where human beings affirm their own self-worth and value in a world where human life seems expendable. This seems to be the pervasive climate of today's world making Tillich's philosophy relevant for our consideration.

In the Hebrew scriptures, this courage to be is derived from and has as its foundation in the answer God gave Moses when asked by the Israelites, "Who do you say you are?" Moses is given the response from God as, "I am who am," that is, *I am Being* (Exodus 3:14). The courage to be is the inherent drives of living and safeguarding one's existence. It is the ultimate power of the self.

The courage to be is not just a metaphysical concept or philosophical exigency but also our very lives. Humans are humans solely because they have the potential of being in relationship with other human beings.

In Shakespearean terminology in the words of Hamlet, "to be or not to be" is not solely the question or an option, but "to be" is the core courage of our living and the cause of all our decisions and behaviors.

In the Hebrew language, the word *faithfulness* implies not just being committed but also *being what you are supposed to be!* It means fidelity and consistency in expecting people to act as their nature would normally act if evil never interfered. Being faithful and having consistent goodness in one's behavior should be as normal as breathing; to stop breathing spells death, and to stop being with the courage in one's convictions is fatal.

In summary, we have highlighted at least six characteristics of what self-transformation entails. It is built on faith as human reality and divine mystery. It is a generosity of spirit, which is boundless.

It is the humility to accept oneself while at the same time accepting others for who they are despite our differences. It demands transparency and honesty in relationship. It involves conversion and self-reclamation. It is ultimately the courage to be *as* Oneself interacting with the world. It is being present to another and being real in the here and now.

Self-transformation defies the use of gimmicks to change one's direction in life. It defies utilizing mere behavioral modifications to change one's attitude in living. Self-transformation is hard work done over a significant period of time, which involves sacrifice, commitment, and risk to accept and put into action specific human values, not a quick fix or trade-off to obtain a needed effect. It is not born of compromise but of faith. It is a process to reform one's life from self-centeredness to being open to altruism, utilizing life received in relationships.

It is losing one's life in generosity and goodness in order to find oneself.

It is not confined to losing oneself by forfeiting monetary or material gains but losing oneself by clearly defining one's limitations, priorities, strengths, agendas, and faults to be an effective communicator and bridge builder of community.

Self-transformation involves a change of heart, not preoccupied with what technique is more effective in making one a better person. Altruism trumps behavioral or cosmetic changes to acquire a needed effect. Self-transformation admits to accepting change as a reality of life and adjustment to what the technology of the day brings, not merely change for change's sake or change because it is the mode of the day. As one ages, it is more difficult to change one's ways or leave our settled ways. In fact, as we advance in age, I ask myself, "Why does time goes so fast when I am moving so slow?" Self-transformation becomes both the energy and power of self-affirmation. It is to be true to oneself, which is the courage to be while always embracing the truth, justice, and righteousness. It is always dealing with what reality presents us. My truth needs to be reconciled with what the truth is. My opinion needs to be in concert and grounded with the facts of existence. If I stray from this, I will eventually become irrelevant in time because my life will be driven by sheer subjectivism and in turn lose grounding in reality. Many times, reality is unpleasant and not the sexy thing to be involved with, or even cruel, but I need to acknowledge it in making life decisions and not act in a vacuum or live in a glass menagerie of self-delusion.

If I were to define, outline, and give a visual representation of the relationship of faith to self-transformation and in turn to redemption, it would be seen as follows:

*Faith.* The inherent natural human drive to seek the assurance of realities hoped for; the conviction of things not visibly seen.

*Goal of faith as human reality.* To discover and actualize one's potential to integrate the self by harmonizing with other humans and being at peace with the world.

*Goal of faith as divine mystery.* To live in accordance to truth, justice, and righteousness utilizing religious traditions to seek communion with the Divine (God).

*Self-transformation.* The work of conversion and self-reformation. It is the radical turning away from self-centeredness to self-giving.

*Redemption.* Saving process where humans reach their ultimate goal in life. In human terms, redemption is the justification of internalizing one's altruistic goals that make life worth living. In divine terms, redemption is only possible via divine intervention, allowing humanity to attain the final goal of eternal life.

| FAITH + | SELF-TRANSFORMATION = | REDEMPTION |
|---|---|---|
| Anchored in relationship | Radical change in behavior | Saving process |
| One's ultimate concern | Courageous movement from self-centeredness to being other-directed | Communion of life and love<br><br>Self-actuation consummation of life's goals |
| "Believing in" another | Time-conditioned process of conversion/reformation | Achieving full humanity<br>Final destination—eternal bliss |

| | | |
|---|---|---|
| Spirit groping for freedom | Process of self-acclamation | |
| Believing w/o the evidence | Recognition/owning of one's feelings | |
| Soul-searching journey | Cognitive restructuring to see situations in perspective and in context with reality | |
| Conviction and hope in what is not visibly seen | Transition from self-concern to empathy for others<br><br>Freedom to seek the truth by checking out one's truth with reality and the facts of life | |
| Inherent human drive | Anchored in justice and righteousness | |
| Free gift not earned or deserved | Goal-oriented behavior | |

# Demons, the Daimonic and the Angel

Have they no refuge or resource? Are there no prisons? Are there
no workhouses?… I don't make merry myself at Christmas,
and I can't afford to make idle people merry. If they rather die,
they had better do it, and decrease the surplus population.

—Ebenezer Scrooge

The four pillars of self-destruction and the antithesis of self-transformation are self-indulgence, abuse of power, narcissism, and hypocrisy. These behaviors are the demons of our time and, for that matter, any time. We can minimize their harmful effects by all sorts of psychobabble rationalizations, but the fact remains they are all demeaning of what it means to be fully human.

Self-indulgence is the excessive use of objects that are good in themselves but used for sheer pleasure in a hedonistic manner that deteriorate the dignity of the human person. Formerly, self-indulgence was identified with hedonism of classical Greece with the practice of the Epicureans. Some of these objects of pleasure include wealth, food, drink (alcohol), drugs, sex, or positions of influence or affluence. All these things are good in themselves. It is how they are used in self-indulgence that is at issue. Self-indulgence is not just exclusive self-gratification but basically greed, avarice, and the decadent use of what is good. There is no empathy where greed exists. An example of this would be if one drives a vehicle while intoxicated with alcohol for merely self-pleasure without reflecting upon the possible consequences of putting oneself and others at risk or if one is engaging in promiscuous sex with another despite having a covert contagious disease.

Self-indulgence has also been manifested by many of our professional athletes where multimillion-dollar players have an insatiable drive to earn even more to satisfy their egos to be the player who earns the most. This mindset is usually followed with the comment made by the athlete to their fans and those who cover the respective sport with, "Well, I need to feed my family" or "I need to get the most I can because who knows if I am no longer able to play after today because of injury."

I know we live in a capitalistic society where one can earn as much as one wants, but my question is, how much is enough, enough? It would appear one would more than have an abundance to feed generations of one's family. I am intrigued when that comment is made by athletes about worrying to feed their families, wondering what are they eating—platinum? I realize that these athletes are the best in the world in what they do, but when enough is never enough, we call that greed. It seems analogous to Ebenezer Scrooge's attitude toward the needy—"It's not my business… It's enough for a man to understand his own business, and not to interfere with other people's. Mine occupies me constantly…" (stave 1—"Marley's Ghost"). One's constant preoccupation with wealth is greed. This is the self-indulgence I am talking about.

Abuse of power is another evil. This behavior is the exploitation of the rights, freedoms, and dignity of others. It includes the accumulation or use of wealth or power at the cost of exploiting others for sheer profit and fame. We have seen this play out in the theater of sexual harassment in the workplace and with assault, human trafficking, and compromising people by the abuse of power by those in authority using status or entitlement to make others subservient. This travesty in society is evident everywhere from the greatest crime of human trafficking to inappropriate sexual remarks made to a coworker.

Narcissism is the third dehumanizing evil that is psychiatrically classified as a serious personality disorder. It is grossly self-centered behavior having excessive interest in one's physical appearance and excessive occupation with one's own needs, often at the expense of others. It showcases not only self-absorption but an indifference toward the needs of others. It has to do with the complete insulation from reality and obliviousness toward the sensitivities of people.

It is characterized by a lack of empathy due to entitlement and an excessive need for self-admiration. A good current example of this disorder is evident in the world of the Academy Awards of Motion Pictures, where the history of annual awards evening had been always a celebration of the work of skilled and talented artists in the world of motion pictures. Most recently, it has degraded to being solely a celebration of the celebrity and wealth of actors.

The main focus nowadays seems to center upon the lifestyles of the rich and famous as glorified by social media and at times engaging in aggressive competition with fellow actors instead of valuing their achievements for the promotion of the industry. Having been a fan of the Academy Awards since the 1960s, I find myself no longer one due to the numerous undercurrent political agendas in recent productions along with the ostentatious display of fame where the glitter of diversified lifestyles of actors overshadows the reason for the awards, which is to celebrate and promote the industry of motion pictures. Has this not become a narcissistic showcase? Has it not betrayed its chartered purpose of being a celebration of the achievement of incredible actors and the industry of motion pictures?

Hypocrisy is the fourth demon, which is defined as one not conforming to one's claim of having high moral standards or beliefs. It is pretense and the lack of transparency in relationship with others. This evil seems to be growing in society exponentially. This is clearly evident in our present-day political landscape where politicians, government officials, and lawmakers lie in clear sight even when confronted by evidence brought to their attention against them. They remain nontransparent and steadfast in their deceit or denial while continuing to believe that the public will continue to trust their good intentions and disregard their duplicity.

All four demons plague our culture and are rampant in the "me generation" mindset of "selfies," which does not quite promote human growth, let alone self-transformation. The paradox of self-transformation is that it only thrives when it is "other directed" rather than when it is used for self-entitlement.

You may say that these four social demons, which are not uncommon, correspond to and are rooted in the traditional Christian understanding of the five capital sins—pride, greed, wrath, envy, lust, gluttony, and sloth. And you would be correct. The unfortunate reality is that these nemeses of self-transformation all have in common the degradation of good things. For example, personal pride, which motivates one to be competitive, professional, and promote one's self-esteem so as to become an autonomous self, is a good thing. However, when this ambition becomes self-righteousness with the drive to control others for self-gain, it is sheer conceit and abusive manipulation. Wealth or money is a good thing. People earn it from their labors and deserve the fruit of their productivity. However, when the acquisition of wealth becomes the ultimate concern of life and the love of money takes precedence over the value of people, it becomes the source of greed and self-indulgence with the potential of becoming sheer decadence. The objects of food, drink (including alcohol), human sexuality, legal gambling, and the legal use of drugs and the responsible use of prescribed medications of themselves are all good things, but when they are used in excess to abuse oneself or others, they become lustful, gluttonous, harmful, and destructive. They no long promote self-transformation but become the masters of slavery in the form of addiction and human vice.

The power of self-affirmation, which is the courage to exercise one's voice, is an important ingredient of self-transformation. However, when it strays and promotes the good of oneself at the cost of exploiting others, it no longer becomes virtuous but narcissistic. The object of leadership and administration of goods in our society is a very noble human endeavor, but when it takes the road of hypocrisy to play the game of politics, or the pursuit of the lust for power or wealth and lacks transparency in dealing with others, it leads to distrust, pretense, and deceit.

The life struggle between self-indulgence and self-transformation where the antagonist becomes the protagonist is the story of Ebenezer Scrooge. This is the crux of *A Christmas Carol.* This was the life struggle Dickens himself experienced in writing this Christmas novella in dealing with the culture he was familiar with where he created *A Christmas Carol.* His times in London during the Victorian Age characterized the socioeconomic gap between *the haves* and have-nots, between the luxurious rich and the destitute with little room for the middle working class caught in the middle, no pun intended. Sounds familiar? It seems to describe our society today and increasingly becoming the trend where the rich become richer and the poor become poorer with the middle class mostly paying the freight. Social change, which is the outcry today, was also that message of Dickens's masterpiece.

What is the life project we call self-transformation all about? Self-transformation has as its prime directive to be creative, natural, transparent, and free. So it translates to, if living is without human freedom of choice, it lacks creativity, and where there is no creativity, there is no life. To determine its creative force and the beauty of self-transformation, one needs to examine closely the struggle and tension between two powerful realities of existence: the daimonic (demonic) and the angelic reality of human love. The simple acts of basic human virtue, i.e., compassion, forgiveness, prayer, understanding, loyalty, and loving affection, make all the differences between heaven and hell, life and death, angelic or demonic possession. The history of civilization throughout time has always been about the tension between the angelic acts of love versus daimonic possession. The theater of strife has always been characterized by sex and eros, anger and rage, and craving for power and lust for wealth. All these have the potential to enslave the whole person. Daimonic possession is not so much diabolic possession but when any natural human function has the power to take over the whole person. This sounds similar to what happens with addiction, but in this case, we are not talking about the nature of a disease but the deliberate choice, freedom, and willingness to live and love. Freedom to choose is not a free gift. It is not entitlement or given by birthright but earned through being knowledgeable, responsible, courageous, just, and respectful of the rights and needs of others and respect for oneself.

The term *daimonic*, from which we get the word *demonic*, is derived from the Greek word *daimon*, meaning a "supernatural being" or "spirit." It originally meant a spiritual being that influenced a person's character or a deity or divine power, lesser god, guiding spirit, one's genius, lot or fortune, not necessarily an evil force. In the thirteenth century, it took on the meaning of "an evil spirit," malignant supernatural being, or a devil from the Latin daemon "spirit."

The life struggle of love versus the *daimonic* is the story of human civilization, the perennial struggle between good and evil. It is the struggle of the angel versus the *daimonic*. It is the arduous task for humanity to seek courage to reclaim itself. The *daimonic* is not necessarily the supernatural evil spirit but any natural function or human instinct that has the power to take over the whole person and not allow a human being to reclaim oneself.[43]

*Daimonic* is synonymous with terms such as *demonic* (popularized form) or *daemonic* (a term used by poets in medieval times). When this power goes awry and one element usurps control over the total personality, we have "daimon possession," the traditional name in psychiatry throughout history for psychosis.[44] The *daimon* only becomes evil when it usurps the total self without regard to the integration of that self or usurps the desires of others and their need for integration. This power may appear as excessive aggression, hostility, cruelty—those behaviors that we are ashamed of or horrify ourselves. Many times, we repress these forbidden impulses or project them on others so as not to lose control. The *daimonic* is that which is raw instinct sometimes described as animal instinct and at times unruly in us. To give an example how the *daimonic* works in humans, we can turn to a case study in psychotherapy as described by renowned psychoanalyst Rollo May, who was a training and supervisory analyst at the William Alanson White Institute of Psychiatry, Psychoanalysis and Psychology.[45]

Possession by a state not commonly considered daimonic as such—namely, loneliness is a good example. In this patient, attacks of acute loneliness developing into panic were not infrequent. He could not orient himself in the panic, could not hang on to his sense of time, and became, as long as the bout of loneliness lasted, numb to his reactions to the world. The ghostlike character of this loneliness was shown in the fact that it could vanish instantaneously with a ring on the phone or his hearing the step of someone coming down the hall. He tried desperately to fight off these attacks, as we all do, which is not surprising since acute loneliness seems to be the most painful kind of anxiety that a human being can suffer. Patients often tell us that the pain is a physical gnawing in their chest or feels like the cutting of a razor in their heart region, as well as a mental state of feeling like an infant abandoned in a world where nobody exists. This particular patient would try, when the loneliness began, to wrench his mind away to thoughts about something else, to get busy doing work, or to go out to a movie, but no matter what escape he tried, there remained the haunting satanic menace hovering behind him like a hated presence waiting to plunge a rapier into his lungs. If he were working, he could practically hear the Mephistophelean laugh behind him mocking him with the reminder that his stratagem would not succeed; sooner or later, he would have to stop, more fatigued than ever, and immediately would come the rapier. Or if he were in the movies, the awareness couldn't be suppressed every time the scene changed that this gnawing ache would come back again as soon as he stepped out on the street. But one day, he came in reporting that he had made a surprising discovery. When an acute attack of loneliness was beginning, it occurred to him not to try and fight it off—running had never helped anyway. Why not accept it, breathe with it, turn toward it and not away? Amazingly, the loneliness did not overwhelm him when he confronted it directly. Then it seemed to diminish. Emboldened, he began to invite it by imagining situations in the past when he was acutely lonely, the memories of which had, up to now, always been sure to cue off the panic. But strangely enough, the loneliness had lost its power. He couldn't feel the panic even when he tried. The more he turned on it and welcomed it, the more impossible it was even to imagine how he'd ever been lonely in the unbearably painful way before.[46]

It is interesting to know that the patient experienced acute loneliness only when he ran from it, but when he turned on it and confronted it with courage as if it were metaphorically a diabolic experience, it vanished. The very act of running away is a response that assures the *daimonic* of its obsessive power. This is the evil of daimonic possession, not so much as being controlled by a diabolical force per se but when anxiety, loneliness, or "abandoned anxiety" being at its most painful overcomes the individual to the extent that the person loses orientation in the objective world. By losing perspective and relationship with the world is to lose one's self and vice versa.

This is the evil of the *daimonic*. This is the perennial struggle to tame the *daimonic* in one's life when it causes one to lose the ability to integrate oneself, resulting in being detached from oneself as well as with the world around them. Existentially, this is what nonbeing means, not just the loss of one's existence but losing one's grounding in reality. Even if this doesn't result in psychosis, it brings into one's life the horror of loss of self, which goes beyond the typical identity crisis experienced in adolescence. Once there is a loss of self, there is a loss of love. There is a loss of relationship. There is a loss of connection with the world. For the existentialist, this is nonbeing or the loss of being. Tragically, this is the loss of meaning in life.

This is the evil pervasiveness of what nonbeing is in the sense of the loss of one's self and loss of being grounded in reality. It does not necessarily mean satanic possession but psychiatric trauma and, emotionally, emptiness and, spiritually, the experience of nothingness. One integrates the self by being grounded in the real via self-awareness and self-consciousness, allowing for an accountability for how one behaves. This is what being is—the courage to exist and stand in the world autonomously in relationship to it. It is a stance one takes in actively living and interacting with the world, not merely being content with passive survival.

The constructive side and lesson learned in the case study presented views a patient enveloped by loneliness who is a gifted, intelligent, and talented person who had achieved success in practically all realms of human experience but failed to use one's capacities to have a relationship with others, that is, unable to open oneself to the world. The patient's growing self-preoccupation with anxiety hindered him to share feelings and trust others. In short, he lacked and desperately needed the exercise of his capacities to love and have an active, outgoing concern for others' welfare—that is human empathy.

The *daimonic* derailed his ability in sharing both the pleasure and delight as an individual with the other for a communion of consciousness and presence with his fellow human beings. He allowed the *daimonic* to rob his potentiality for active loving, losing meaning in his life. The *daimonic* depleted his potential to enjoy and have intimate experience with another. This is what it means to be truly present to another. The power of presence of the interaction of human beings comes into play not just by doing for others but "being" for others. When this doesn't occur, we have what we call existentially nonbeing.

The *daimonic* is at the root of the four demons identified earlier in this chapter, which hinder self-transformation. The *daimonic* doesn't allow for second chances but stunts one in its journey for self-transformation. It is an inclination toward self-centeredness and self-absorption. It is surrendering to the animal instinct of fight-or-flight behavior. It is the inclination toward the raw and an uncontrollable drive for self-satisfaction. When it fully takes hold of a person, it may lead to emotional dysfunction or disintegration of the self.

The *daimonic* is what Sigmund Freud attributes to be implicit in his emphasis on "fate" and "destiny." It is associated with his many psychoanalytic concepts such as libido, which he sees as an impulsive and instinctive drive that resides in the self and can seize one and render us as "nature's tool" that can overpower one's judgment and, if not managed by the ego (the self's executive function), could lead to pathology. This impulsive instinct of the libido is identified as one of the human passions called eros. It is the basic primitive need to want what one wants when one wants it and as much as one wants. It is the first stage of psychosexual development found in an infant. The infant is totally dependent upon the caregiver but acts on "pure id"— that is, the infant wants what it wants when it wants it for as long as it wants. For Freud, the *daimonic* is identified as eros when one speaks of one type of human passion, this being the passion for sex.

The opposing power of the *daimonic* such as eros (sheer lust) would be the angelic reality of love as self-giving. Treatment or cure for the *daimonic* is not an exorcism of an evil spirit but self-transformation and ability to share love with another, not sheer possession of the other by loving. The *daimonic* is not angelic love but selfish dominance and possession. Human existence is the life struggle of the *daimonic* versus this kind of love. The type of selfless love becomes the angel in our lives, which gives life. Similar to the attributes of an angel love is timeless, spiritual, eternal, noncorporeally based, life-giving, and leads to communion of beings. This love is the courage to stand up for the self and take the needed responsible risks to reach out and empathize with other human beings. It is manifested in human acts of faith, trust, patience, kindness, empathy, compassion, humility, hope, and self-giving. A solid description of this angelic reality of love as compared to the passion of love as lust (eros) as the *daimonic* purports is beautifully described by Paul the Apostle in the Christian scriptures.

> If I speak in the tongues of men, [women] and of angels, but have not love, I am a noisy gong or a clanging cymbal. And if I have prophetic powers, and understand all mysteries and all knowledge, and if I have all faith, so as to remove mountains, but have not love, I am nothing. If I give away all I have and if I deliver my body to be

burned, but have not love, I gain nothing. Love is patient and kind; love is not jealous or boastful, it is not arrogant or rude. Love does not insist on its own way; it is not irritable or resentful; it does not rejoice at wrong, but rejoices in the right. Love bears all things, believes all things, hopes all things, endures all things.

Love never ends; as for prophesies, they will pass away, as for tongues, they will cease; as for knowledge, it will pass away. For our knowledge is imperfect and our prophecy is imperfect; but when the perfect comes, the imperfect will pass away. When I was a child, I spoke like a child, I thought like a child, I reasoned as a child; when I became a man, I gave up childish ways. For now, we see in a mirror dimly, but then face to face. Now I know in part; then I shall understand fully, even as I have been fully understood. So, faith, hope, love abide, these three; but the greatest of them is love. (1 Corinthians 13:1–13)

Every person, experiencing as one does his or her own solitariness and aloneness, longs for union with another. He or she yearns to participate in a relationship greater than oneself. Ordinarily, one strives to overcome one's aloneness through some form of love. Whether it be friendship, carnal union, or steadfast family loyalty, love becomes that union that allows one to find oneself by self-giving and surrendering to another. When it becomes self-centered exclusive raw pleasure, it no longer is angelic love and life-giving but mere carnal desire, lust, and concupiscence that is solely a desire of the flesh. It is the *daimonic* at work. The same is true of other human passions such as the lust for wealth or power or fame.

In our discussion of *A Christmas Carol,* which seems to have gotten lost in these pages of philosophical thought and psychological study of human behavior, it is the lust for wealth and the power of affluence through material gain that focuses our attention on Ebenezer Scrooge. He personifies the world of the *daimonic* as it is a disregard for humanity and the angelic nature of love. He is the symbol of where the world has gone wrong and cold to human sensibilities and eternal values. He is the personification not only of selfishness and conceit but also of overindulgence, narcissism, hypocrisy, and the abuse of power.

Scrooge's overindulgence is manifested by greed and avarice where money becomes his god. He is narcissistic in the sense that he takes pleasure in his accumulation of wealth as a successful businessman indifferent to the needs of others. He is an abuser of power by exploiting his clients whom he lends money to and also demeans his sole employee, Bob Cratchit. Finally, he is hypocritical and deceitful in the sense that he takes pride in being a prominent citizen of society while gloating over his supposedly support of the poor and destitute of London by involuntarily supporting the system that keeps the union workhouses and prisons in operations as well as maintaining the full vigor of the treadmill and the Poor Law.[47]

The treadmill found in numerous English prisons in Dickens's time was a rotating wooden cylinder, large in diameter and wide, formed of steps deep enough to allow criminal prisoners to tread continuously as if walking up steps. This activity was a punishment prescribed in a prisoner's sentence. When first instituted, the treadmill served no useful purpose, but in later years, it was adapted such that the prisoners' constant stepping would drive a shaft in order to grind corn, pump water, or perform some other function of a mill.[48] "The Poor Law" refers to periodically modified legislation, originating in the fourteenth century and modified in 1834 and after the 1843 publication of *A Christmas Carol,* to provide relief for the poor, though in effect, the law stigmatized destitution. These union workhouses were established pursuant to the Poor Law. A fundamental principle of the Poor Law held that able-bodied persons should perform work in exchange for public assistance and, if unemployed, therefore, should be confined to a workhouse rather than receiving "outside relief."[49]

Inmates were allowed to discharge themselves with notice to authorities. Many times, operators of these workhouses skimped on food in order to pocket a portion of the funds that were allocated for the sustenance of inmates, one reason that the conditions of these "death traps" was particularly appalling. This was prime motivation for Charles Dickens to bring to light the evils of social injustice, which became evident in his classic novel *Oliver Twist*. Along with the deplorable conditions of how these people lived and worked in these workhouses was the ineffective legislation of the Poor Law, which was aimed to help the poor but instead contributed in making poverty essentially inescapable. Charles Dickens was a fierce public critic of both.

In summary, the struggle between the power of the daimonic and the angelic reality of love can be reframed as the contest between misery and mercy, between the raw instinct of self-gratification versus altruistic love. In his novel *Dr. Fischer of Geneva*, Graham Greene explores two competing forces in human life—self-respect and greed. The protagonist in the novel, Dr. Fischer, is a man who has made his mission in life of treating others with open contempt. Dr. Fischer has made his millions from a toothpaste that controls the decay caused by eating too many Swiss chocolates. He goes out of his way to surround himself with people whom he delights to tease and torment. In fact, at his luxurious parties, he plays on his guests' greed by offering them luxurious gifts if they submit themselves to his humiliations. These guests play along winning these expensive gifts by accepting the insults for the sake of the gifts. They lose the little self-respect they have left. In fact, they keep coming back again and again to these parties. Dr. Fischer sees himself made in the image and likeness of a God who gives presents and makes bribes in between the humiliations he inflicts on others. He sort of has power over his guests, a power that dehumanizes them, a power that causes them to lose themselves and their relationship with the world. It is the power of the daimonic where the self loses its orientation and perspective of the world. The self no longer lives in a real world but in a menagerie of its own making where authentic meaning in life has been evaporated and replaced with the misery that comes from self-centeredness. That is what happened to Dr. Fischer's guests. They lost themselves in their attempt to satisfy their primitive drives. These primitive drives take the forms of wealth, sex, fame, and power over others. This is the world of the daimonic.

On the other hand, the world of altruistic love takes on the dimension of mercy, forgiveness, and acceptance of others as they are not as one would have them. With love, there is no power exerted over them but only empowerment of others to love. Misery has been replaced by human empathy, tenderness, and mercy. The point about mercy is that nobody deserves it. Everyone deserves true justice; mercy on the other hand is sheer gift. Mercy cancels out wrongs and transgressions, not because a sparkling defense has been discovered or excusing causes have been skillfully argued but because that is the free response of the person who is grieved or wronged. Mercy does not suggest that the guilty are not guilty; it recognizes the guilt but does not demand satisfaction for the wrong. In all this, mercy reflects the utter graciousness of the one who has been wronged.

A story is told of a young French soldier who deserted Napoleon's army but who, within a matter of hours, was caught by his own troops as a traitor. To discourage soldiers from abandoning their posts, the penalty for desertion was death. The young soldier's mother heard what had happened and went to plead with Napoleon to spare the life of her son. Napoleon heard her plea but pointed out that because of the serious nature of the crime her son had committed, he clearly didn't deserve mercy. "I know he doesn't deserve mercy," the mother answered. "It wouldn't be mercy if he deserved it." That is the whole nature of the angelic reality of love along with mercy; one doesn't deserve it, for it is sheer gift.

Similar to mercy, forgiveness, tenderness, and human empathy, love is the antidote to the daimonic. Demons and the daimonic fall in the sight of the angelic reality of love. That is why self-transformation cannot happen without it. That was the missing link in Scrooge's life—he couldn't accept being forgiven by his father. He was not capable of demonstrating mercy to those whom he felt wronged him, and he couldn't love because he allowed the daimonic to take possession of his life. Hence, Scrooge found no resource in loving and forgiving. The workhouses and prisons became his defense toward anyone in need who asked from him any human tenderness and compassion. He cannot make merry at Christmas because he lacked the patience, generosity, and willingness to risk his vulnerability to share with others. So he settled for apathy and indifference toward those who couldn't benefit his cause for profit, in his own words—"I can't afford to make idle people merry…so they had better die and decrease the surplus population." The voice of Scrooge was the voice of the daimonic.

# Transformation as Therapeutic Process

---

I am here to-night to warn you that you have yet the chance and hope of escaping my fate… You will be haunted by Three Spirits… without their visits you cannot hope to shun the path I tread.
—Marley to Scrooge

There are two important dimensions of self-transformation when it comes to understanding it in the context of *A Christmas Carol*. They are time and the role of dreams in the human psyche. Time becomes a significant marker in Scrooge's three ghost visits. Time becomes Scrooge's hourglass for him to change his ways. Oddly enough, Scrooge's ghostly apparitions get condensed into a night's odyssey of timelessness covering his entire life. Dickens goes to great lengths to insist that the apparent three dreams are not dreams at all but real events in the life of a morally impoverished rich man. They are three parables of how a grumpy, squeezing, wrenching, grasping, scraping, clutching, covetous old miser was able to transform into a righteous person. This transformation came about via "the nocturnal escapees" of one man's life from being a sinner to being graced and blessed. Scrooge undergoes conversion in these dreams with anxiety, trepidation, and sheer belief in a hope of escaping death but never at any time really certain that he will be saved.

Only one condition can free him from this apparent purgatory, which his partner Jacob Marley had foretold—*humankind, not wealth, is to be his business.* Marley's earlier apparition was an admonition for Scrooge that what awaited him was a wasteland of endless purgatory. Scrooge witnessed this vividly upon his encounter with Marley's ghost, which disappeared into the night where the air was filled with chained spirits, many he recognized as figures from his past who had not regretted their actions in time. Dickens sets Scrooge up as the quintessential sinner and most miserable of men. Dickens universalizes the message of the sin of self-righteousness not only as pertaining to Scrooge's life alone but also to all who allow business to devalue the human person.

This is not solely a tale of one man's redemption but a social ultimatum to society to make business work for humanity, not humanity work for business.

Time is indeed our only measure of our accomplishments in this life no matter how much goodwill is shown. Time is the most precious commodity we own. In fact, it is not a commodity but a necessity in life. In the motion picture *Gone with the Wind*, there is a scene early in the story where there is a sundial outside one of the establishments that reads, "Do not squander time. It is the stuff life is made of." Time is fleeting, and it quickly unfolds the stories of our lives. The concept of time is a theme that runs throughout the novella. Scrooge is haunted by ghosts of his past, present, and future. In this Christmas tale, there are bells chiming and clocks tolling, reminding Scrooge of the passage of time. The chain that Marley bears reminds Scrooge of an endless prison sentence with its unmelodious and piercing sound.

The second significant element utilized by Dickens in his Christmas novella is the role of dreams in the process of self-transformation.

I think Dickens's purpose of incorporating in detail the apparitions of the spirits during Scrooge's sleep were not so much to give an interpretation of Scrooge's unconscious struggles but rather to make him more reflective of the events in Scrooge's life so as to give him a second chance in retrieving a meaningful existence. The dream becomes the vehicle where transformation is made possible rather than an interpretation of Scrooge's unconscious struggles. In a sense, the dreams make for timelessness where Scrooge is forced to make good decisions from his own free will, and of his own free will, he transforms from a mean penny-pinching miser to a generous bene-factor. Up to this point, this was the road less travelled by Scrooge, which viscerally eats away at him and commands his attention as the dreams unfold.

Whether you are a fan or not of Sigmund Freud's theory of the interpretation of dreams in understanding the world of the uncon-scious mind is not the issue here but rather Dickens's clever use of the dream scenario as a sort of *deus ex machina*. This literary device, which translated in English from the Latin means "God out of a machine," is derived from ancient Greek theater where in a fiction or drama, there appears or is introduced suddenly and unexpectedly a contrived solution to an apparently insoluble difficulty. In this case, how does Dickens reconcile the untenable situation of his day in Victorian London where social injustice runs rampant with his desire to promote and advocate the celebratory spirit of Christmas amid a society tainted by puritanic skepticism of the religiosity of Christmas? Even more challenging, how does Dickens promote his relatively new outlook of Christmas merriment and serenity exhib-ited in family festivities where his main character is so anti-Christ-mas? The answer is, Dickens creates the dream scenario to be a *deus ex machina* to create the possibility of second chances so as to trans-form a miserable, wretched and self-centered sinner to become a con-genial gentleman of faith.

In attempting to understand how Dickens uses the dream motif in his work, it may be beneficial to understand the world of dreams. What I have researched about the purpose of dreams in conjunction with sleep is that it is a psychoneurological phenomenon allowing us to be healthy and functioning well where the body and brain repair, restore, and reenergize. If you don't get adequate amount of sleep, you may experience side effects such as poor memory and focus, weakened immunity, and mood changes.

There are five hypothetical reasons why we sleep: (a) the dream activity in sleep clears the mind of "junk," i.e., clears out toxins from the brain; (b) sleep strengthens important memories and discards useless information; (c) deep sleep allows body tissues to repair themselves; (d) sleep allows the body to conserve energy; and (e) sleep has evolved to the point that it helps hide from predators. The energy conservation theory posits that the main function of sleep is to reduce a person's energy demand during part of the day and night when it is least efficient to hunt for food. This theory is supported by the fact that the body has decreased metabolism by up to 10 percent during sleep.[50] Considering that most of us sleep about one-third of our life span, it isn't surprising that Dickens would employ this human activity to unravel his protagonist story by use of the dream. So too from the psychological ramifications of dreams which occur in REM sleep, they are useful in therapy to understand or disclose unconscious traumas so as to bring to light and hopefully treat issues that many times underlie emotional pain and mental health illnesses.

Although Scrooge did not seek a psychoanalyst to interpret his dreams, it is important to note that dreams are unique of the human experience insofar as they are helpful to maintain restful sleep. They also are of themselves psychotic events of the unconscious during the sleep cycle. They call for specialized interpretation at times to resolve issues when restful sleep is disrupted, e.g., nightmares, night terrors, etc. Debate remains among sleep experts why we dream. Different theories include (a) strengthening memory and informational recall; (b) the way where the brain processes and manages emotions; (c) the brain's way of straightening up and clearing away partial, erroneous, or unnecessary information; (d) dream content may be a form of distorted instant replay where recent events are reviewed and analyzed; or (e) dreaming is just a by-product of sleep with no essential purpose.[51]

Let us take a closer look at *A Christmas Carol* in how cleverly Dickens uses dream as the medium of self-transformation. In stave 1, Scrooge is confronted by the ghost of his former business partner Jacob Marley. However, what initiates Scrooge's process of becoming truly human was his acknowledgment that Jacob was giving him an opportunity to escape the fate of death just as Jacob is experiencing. Dickens makes this evident from Scrooge's interaction with Jacob's ghost from the outset:

Scrooge fell upon his knees, and clasped his hands before his face. "Mercy!" he said. "Dreadful apparition, why do you trouble me?"... To sit staring at those fixed gazed eyes in silence, for a moment, would play, Scrooge felt, the very deuce with him. "It is required of every man," the Ghost returned, "that the spirit within him should walk abroad among his fellow-men, and travel far and wide; and, if that spirit goes not forth in life, it is condemned to do so after death. It is doomed to wander through the world—oh, woe is me!—and witness what it cannot share, but might have shared on earth, and turned to happiness!" Again, the spectre raised a cry, and shook its chain and wrung its shadowy hands. "You are fettered," said Scrooge, trembling. "Tell me why?" "I wear the chain I forged in life," replied the Ghost. *I made it link by link, and yard by yard; I girded it on of my own free-will, and of my own free-will I wore it.* Is its pattern strange to you.?" Scrooge trembled more and more. "Or would you know," pursued the Ghost, "the weight and length of the strong coil you bear yourself? It was full as heavy and as long as this, seven Christmas-eves ago. You have laboured on it since. It is a ponderous chain!" Scrooge glanced about him on the floor, in the expectation of finding himself surrounded by some fifty or sixty fathoms of iron cable, but he could see nothing. "Jacob!" he said imploringly. "Old Jacob Marley. tell me more! Speak comfort to me, Jacob!" "I have none to give.", the Ghost replied." It comes from other regions, Ebenezer Scrooge, and is conveyed by other ministers, to other kinds of men. Nor can I tell you what I would. A very little more is all permitted to me. I cannot rest, I cannot stay, I cannot linger anywhere. My spirit never walked beyond our counting-house-mark me;—in life my spirit never roved beyond the narrow limits of our money-changing hole; and weary journeys lie before me!"... "You must have been very slow about it, Jacob", Scrooge observed in a business-like manner, though with humility and deference. "Slow!" the Ghost repeated. "Seven years dead," mused Scrooge. "And travelling all the time?" "The whole time," said the Ghost. "No rest, no peace. Incessant torture of remorse." "You travel fast? said Scrooge. "On the wings of the wind," replied the Ghost. "You might have got over a great quantity of ground in seven years," said Scrooge.

The Ghost, on hearing this, set up another cry, and clanked its chain so hideously in the dead silence of the night, that the Ward would have been justified in indicting it for nuisance. "Oh! captive, bound and doubled-ironed," cried the phantom, "not to know that ages of incessant labour, by immortal creatures, for this earth must pass into eternity before the good of which it is susceptible is all developed! Not to know that any Christian spirit working kindly in its little sphere, whatever it may be, will find its mortal life too short for its vast means of usefulness! Not to know that no space of regret can make amends for one life's opportunities misused! Yet such was I! Oh, such was I!"

"But you were always a good man of business, Jacob", faltered Scrooge, who now began to apply this to himself. "Business!" cried the Ghost, wringing its hands again. *"Mankind was my business. The common welfare was my business; charity, mercy, forbearance, and benevolence were, all, my business...* "At this time of the rolling year," the spectre said, "I suffer most. Why did I walk through crowds of fellow-beings with my eyes turned down, and never raise them to the blessed Star which led the Wise Men to a poor abode.? Were there no poor homes to which its light would have conducted me?"… "Hear me!" cried the Ghost. "My time is nearly gone."… "I am here to-night to warn you that you have yet a chance and hope of escaping my fate. A chance and hope of my procuring Ebenezer."… "You will be haunted" resumed the Ghost, "by Three Spirits."… *"Without their visits," said the Ghost, "you cannot hope to shun the path I tread."* (Stave 1—"Marley's Ghost")

Ebenezer's persistent resistance to Marley's admonition that he needs to self-reflect where his life has gone allows for the gauntlet to be thrown where Ebenezer is challenged to change his ways now or else. This urgency comes in the form of fear and trepidation. Like many of us, the initial motivation for change and self-transformation is sheer fear. It is this fear of the loss of all those things and some-times individuals in our lives which and who have defined who we are, which ultimately frightens us not to change. Fear leads to panic, which leads to denial, which leads to guilt, which leads to bargaining or compromise, which leads to depression, and hopefully to accep-tance with decision-making and in turn to a change of behavior. This is the cycle of self-transformation.

Like Ebenezer, we are challenged to let go of those things and individuals that have hindered our growth to be caring, loving, and responsible human beings. This is a vital step so as to embrace our own self-reclamation. Scrooge's character development is engineered by Dickens in such a way that Scrooge becomes increasingly aware of his own poverty, lacking in love, warmth, and the spirit of self-giving. As the novella unfolds, we learn that he is an impoverished charac-ter not because of his diminishing wealth, resources, and number of friends but because of his lack of human empathy. His lack of empathy doesn't allow him to forgive and listen to his buried conscience, which ultimately becomes that beacon to seek virtue and goodness in others. A change in that conscience will ultimately be his redemption. This is what it means to be true to Oneself and where Scrooge finds himself.

Stave 2, "The First of the Three Spirits," begins Scrooge's therapeutic journey via the dream to search his soul and find the goodness that is missing or has at least been dormant for many years. This search takes the form of recalling past days, which haunt Scrooge as missed opportunities. Can we say the same of our past, which we no longer can rewrite but only recall? In many cases, the regrets and failures of the past can assist us in writing the present and allow us to hope for better days in the future. However, this was not always the case for Ebenezer Scrooge. He lived in denial and vehemently blocked out his past and remained steadfast in his arrogant spirit. He avoided making changes in the present and ultimately realized that he will die alone and unloved if he continued to treat people the way he did. His only hope was with his encounter with the Spirit of Christmas Yet to Come, it would awaken a sense of remorse so as to desperately change his fate. He goes *mano a mano* in facing death as his last stand to survive eternal perdition.

The journey of Scrooge to progressively eradicate his belief that he has found peace and satisfaction in his own material possessions is first presented by his lonely childhood befuddled by his father's alienation. This resulted in him boarding at school and being left alone during the holidays. It was his sister Fan who came to his rescue to not only mediate his relationship with their father but also to bring him home for Christmas holiday, for she remarked, "Father is so much kinder than he used to be, that home is like Heaven! He spoke so gently to me one dear night when I was going to bed, that I was not afraid to ask him once more if you might come home; and he said Yes, you should…"

The realization that Scrooge's disfavor of Fan's sole child, Fred, Scrooge's nephew, whom he blamed for Fan's death in childbearing, was comparable to Scrooge's father's disfavor of him, blaming Scrooge for his own mother's death during her childbearing (although this is inferred in the tale and not explicitly mentioned).

Another challenge to Scrooge's arrogance is recalled in his past with the generosity of the Fezziwigs, who knew how to conduct festivities for their employees at Christmastime. This sure enough haunted Scrooge, who remembered his ill treatment toward his sole employee, Bob Cratchit, when he remarked, "I should like to be able to say a word or two to my clerk just now, that's all." Next, Scrooge relives reluctantly the breakup of his engagement with Belle, his fiancée, who clearly defined Scrooge's new idol—money, which replaced their love as she remarked to him, "You may—the memory of what is past half makes me hope you will—have pain in this. For a very, very brief time, and you will dismiss the recollection of it gladly, as an unprofitable dream, from which it happened well that you awoke. May you be happy in the life you have chosen!" Challenges to Scrooge's arrogant spirit of his past continues with the vision of experiencing being in a cozy room with the same girl, Belle, now a mother, with her children boisterously celebrating the holiday as Belle's husband enters with his arms full of Christmas gifts. The husband then relates to Belle meeting an old friend of hers earlier. Belle guesses it was Ebenezer, whom her husband tells her that as he passed by Scrooge's office window, he could see a candle burning inside, and he couldn't help but view how Scrooge seemed "alone in the world" as his partner Jacob Marley lies on the point of death. These were the recollections of Scrooge's past, which still did not lessen his self-righteousness and arrogance and did not yet move him to change.

For many of us, do we not act resistantly when our family and friends lovingly encourage us to address our unhealthy behaviors that continue from our past into the present? Do we, like Scrooge, shun them and dismiss them, believing that they really don't not know what we are going through? We attempt desperately to believe they don't really understand us, and so we continue to convince ourselves.

In summary, stave 2 implants the beginnings of the possibility of Scrooge embarking upon a journey of self-transformation. This chapter of his life is characterized only by the past flirting with Scrooge's conscience to take an internal assessment and ask, "Do I still need to be a slave to my demons? To my daimonic? To my idols? Or are there more life-giving possibilities for me to grow as a caring, responsible, and loving human being?" If it could work for Scrooge, it certainly can work for us.

Scrooge's arrogance and intransigence to reform his life continue in stave 3, "The Second of the Three Spirits," as the therapeutic process of self-transformation picks up momentum. What characterizes this stage of Scrooge's journey of soul as described in stave 3 is the possibility to be open to forgiveness and acceptance that one needs forgiveness in order to change. Here Scrooge as a man of business, a man who is overbearing, pompous, and cold, relies solely upon his mind, not his feelings, in all his business transactions. He believes that owning up to one's feelings is a weakness as highlighted at the outset of the story when his nephew announced to him that he's gotten married. Scrooged inquired, "Why?" and Fred responded, "Because I fell in love." Scrooge growled sarcastically, "Because you fell in love, as if that were the only one thing in the world more ridiculous than a merry Christmas."

The Ghost of Christmas Present, like the Spirit of Christmas Past and as we shall see with the Ghost of Christmas Yet to Come, does not follow any set protocol or set script for guiding Scrooge through the journey of transformation. When things don't go as planned, these visions make Scrooge extremely nervous and skeptical about his powers over his world and above all his control over other people's lives. In a weird sort of way, the goodness and authenticity of the people he encounters in these visions influence and confront him with his own mortality.

The Ghost of Christmas Present is the archetypal Father Christmas figure. Scrooge sits as a passive spectator. Unlike his boisterous and argumentative nature, amid the opening scene of stave 3, Scrooge surprisingly exhibits sadness as he encounters the Spirit of Christmas Present, who presents him with a cornucopia of festive, delicious foods, for he couldn't detach himself from his great wealth. His sadness was indicative of his reluctance to seek the light, but he chose to remain in the darkness.

The Ghost of Christmas Present is surprised that Scrooge has not met a spirit like him before because he claims he has more than eighteen hundred brothers [and sisters]. This reference the spirit makes is to show each of the Christmases that have occurred since the birth of Christ—essentially implying how Scrooge seems never to have really experienced a true Christmas. The fact that Scrooge for the first time acknowledges by saying that the previous spirit's lesson is "working now" suggests that he is finding some value with these visions even though they are painful and offensive to his egotistical nature. Scrooge's definition of what is valued in life or, in his own words, "profit" is taking on another meaning beyond monetary wealth. Scrooge begins to become skeptical about his lifestyle and yet at the same time refuses to admit that he needs to reform.

This spirit's special power to have the magical ability fit into any space or room despite his giant size symbolizes how Christmas can be found in any life situation by myriads of different people whether rich or poor. This is especially the sense when the spirit brings Scrooge to witness how the Cratchits prepare the family dinner with merriment and cheer despite their economic impoverished situation. Dickens particularly emphasizes the kindness of this spirit and the manner the spirit favors the poor with his incense that he sprinkles over the town to demonstrate how the virtues of Christmastime are in the poor population but also how those poor are neglected by the charity of the living. I think we all can take a lesson from this as we celebrate Christmas annually with friends and family, realizing that these celebrations are all but a small token of the many blessings we have all received throughout the year. These blessings we revel in unfortunately are not shared by everyone.

In discussing the families that struggle in poverty, our attention goes to the Cratchits. It is not just Bob Cratchit who is the breadwinner that supports this family, but the eldest children Martha and Master Peter are expected to work just as hard. This was a persistent theme focused in Dickens's works where the exploitation and parentification of Victorian children was a real concern where their childhood was transient and not enjoyed but sped up into adulthood. Certainly, Dickens could relate to this from his own childhood. Yet with all the societal abuse of child labor and London's poverty, which had caused a generation of lost childhoods, Dickens describes the Cratchits as imbued with love and joy. Tiny Tim's stature is made fragile and smaller than a typical child his age for the purpose of emphasizing the disparity between his small means and his tremendous spirit.

Scrooge's brief reflection of the new meaning of profit here is crystalized by the fact that Tiny Tim asks God to bless everybody, not just him and his family, showing that he is the antithesis to selfish Scrooge. Yet at the same time, Tim is powerless to improve his situation and condition and will die because those that do have the power to change his fate, like Scrooge, choose not to do so. One of the realities the spirit attempts to demonstrate to Scrooge is the value of knowledge and conscience over ignorance. This was also a primary mission Dickens valiantly promoted by his affiliation with the Manchester Athenaeum to promote education, the arts, and the power of self-determination in human productivity.

Up to this point, Scrooge has been living a closed-minded life, solely focusing on his own financial troubles. Now the scope of his vision as ushered by the Spirit of Christmas Present is widened considerably as he is witnessing what folks who have little have done much and celebrate life with gratitude, song, music, and family gatherings. On Christmas, people always seem to come together in relationship even in the loneliest places, making Scrooge reflect upon how much he has chosen to be alone. As Scrooge and the spirit leave the Cratchit home, they wander together on through the city and witness the wonderful sights where so many people are on their way to visit family. Scrooge can only reflect on, *Where is my family?* The Spirit of Christmas Present rejoices over Scrooge's insight, and he accompanies Scrooge to a faraway deserted moor where miners live, and Scrooge witnesses them seated beside a fire singing songs with their families. Scrooge is amazed to see the joviality of people again who have little but possess a basic human kindness.

The tour with the Spirit of Christmas Present concludes with Scrooge being brought to his nephew's home where he and his wife are hosts celebrating Christmas with games, music, and dinner. Despite the disparaging jokes made by Fred along with his guests about Scrooge's humbug attitude toward Christmas, the act of their ridicule brings Scrooge in as a presence into the party and shows that he is considered to be part of the family although he cannot interact with them. With frustration, he comes to realize that he is missing out on many pleasant moments, which time cannot replace for him. Time is passing, and he is losing those Hallmark moments of joy and family intimacy. Scrooge momentarily attempting to engage in the festivities has forgotten his grumpy ways and found himself happy and excited but is reminded by the spirit that these are only shadows, not reality, and this happy vision cannot continue because time is running out.

Probably the most striking and dramatic moment of the whole story comes after Scrooge's visit to Fred's festivities, where the spirit uncovers his robe to show Scrooge the vices of ignorance and want personified by two cowering children. The children are poor and ragged, showing how the vices that Scrooge has indulged in—especially ignorance—has a real effect on the children in the workhouses and on the streets. The two figures of Want and Ignorance, sheltering in the robes of the Ghost of Christmas Present, were inspired by the children Dickens had seen on his visit to a ragged school in the East End of London.[52] This, along with touring the Cornish tin mines in 1843, where he was angered by seeing children working in appalling conditions, inspired him to write *A Christmas Carol* in response to

British social attitudes toward poverty, particularly child poverty, and wished to launch this novella to provoke social change.

As Scrooge witnesses this social atrocity victimizing children, it is safe to conclude that Scrooge becomes confused, ambivalent, and disgruntled by the life he has lived and asks to see the future. He is now skeptical of what man he was and begins the process of self-reformation.

# Redemption as Saving Event

Hear me [Spirit] I am not the man I was… Assure me that I may change these shadows you have shown me, by an altered life!
—Scrooge to Ghost of Christmas Yet to Come

The final phrase of Scrooge's repentance and self-atonement to complete his self-transformation comes in the third parable of the ghost visitations—his meeting with the Spirit of Christmas Yet to Come.

Christmas Yet to Come is significantly different than the previous visions insofar as it is a sad, immoral place, full of people who have the same miserly values Scrooge has exhibited in his life. They don't care or even recognize the man who had died; they care similar to Scrooge, only about what they can profit from. Scrooge has been isolated in such a small, selfish world that he doesn't even realize that the businessmen who gather daily at the stock exchange where he often frequented are talking about him. Scrooge is upset of their callous lack of empathy for the dead man but doesn't realize that they are echoing his own cruel phrases and opinions. The dead man of whom they speak was a wealthy selfish individual, a man who might have thought of himself as commanding respect and esteem among his contemporaries and colleagues especially over the poor whom he considered to be inferiors. Yet here Scrooge realizes that for all this man's wealth, the man died alone with no one to remember him or stand up for him, and in fact, he is afforded no respect at all by even the scavengers and dealers whom he used to dismiss. Little did Scrooge realize at this point that the dead man they speak of is him.

The final phrase of this therapeutic process where Scrooge needs to demonstrate sincere remorse for his life of avarice and indifference as exhibited by his cruelty to others is the climax of his repentance and conversion. The vision goes from bad to worse. Scrooge seems to have a sense that the fate he is witnessing in terms of the dead man is his own but still hides behind a veneer of ignorance and denial. As the tale comes to its finale, he becomes more and more distraught with the spirit's lack of sympathy, for there is nothing he can do but watch as his worst fears regarding the dead man are confirmed.

This living horror is confirmed when the spirit takes him to the Cratchit home where the family is unusually silent, waiting for their father to come home. Mrs. Cratchit is sewing but stops because the color is making her eyes tired. As Scrooge enters with the spirit, he hears a phrase as if in a dream. "And he took a child, and set him in the midst of them." Scrooge realizes that Tiny Tim has died. Bob Cratchit is due home, but one of the children says that he's been walking slower recently, and they all agree that he used to walk more quickly with Tiny Tim on his shoulders.

As Bob arrives home, he tells his family of the beautiful kindness rendered by Scrooge's nephew Fred, whom he met in the street upon his return from seeing the plot where Tim will be buried. Fred noticed Bob's grief and gave him sincere condolences with his address so that the family could keep in touch with him if they needed anything.

Bob thinks that Fred might even be able to get Peter, his eldest, a job.

Scrooge continues to grow distraught by these visions and is led by the spirit to a church graveyard. It is here the climax of his dreams and full disclosure that the dead man he witnessed earlier on a bed was him as the spirit pointed out a grave site with Scrooge's own name inscribed on it. Scrooge cries out, knowing that he is the dead man on the bed, alone and unloved. He gets upon his knees before the spirit and begs to reassure him that an altered life will produce an altered fate. Scrooge vows to honor Christmas and learn all his lessons from this therapeutic journey of the soul. Scrooge's ignorance and denial is dissipated when he comes to the understanding that his greed has led him inexorably to the horrible loneliness that he had witnessed in the vision of the future, to a death uncared about by anyone. Faced with this vision and reality, Scrooge begins suddenly and dramatically to repent. Scrooge comes to the understanding that the riches he wedded himself to—to become someone—have betrayed him where now he has become no one.

This is how stave 4 ends and how the therapeutic process of Scrooge finding himself begins.

A new life is rendered to Ebenezer Scrooge, whose self-transformation is complete, and he now is redeemed of all his iniquities. Scrooge's new life begins by awakening from his dream to discover that he had not missed Christmas Day at all. In fact, he thanks the spirits for getting things done in one evening instead of the initial admonition of Marley, which seemed to imply a three-night affair. Scrooge wakes to find himself back in bed, in his rooms, his face wet with tears. Scrooge's awakening from his deep, strange, and prolonged slumber becomes a moment of enlightenment, a complete transformation, a spiritual rebirth.

As the bells start chiming, Scrooge runs to the window and views a beautiful cold winter day. The fog has lifted from the London skies, and the cacophonous sound of church bells fills the air and sets the tone for Scrooge to be reborn. Scrooge momentarily relives childhood as he recalls how wonderful waking up on Christmas morning was. Scrooge is ecstatic not to have missed Christmas Day. He sees a boy from his balcony and asks the boy to go to the nearby market where there is a huge prize turkey in the window. He tells the boy to buy it and offers him half a crown if he comes back quickly. The grateful boy dashes off. As Scrooge waits for the turkey, he sees the door knocker again and exclaims how thankful he is to it for showing him Jacob Marley's face.

This turn of events where Scrooge comes back from the horrors of his past life of futility to a renewed life of generosity, joy, and gratitude is characteristic of what happens in the process of conversion.

What does this turnabout mean in our own lives? Do we recall experiences in our lives where we make a deliberate choice to leave one path and seek another even though it may be uncertain and unpopular but puts us in a healthier, safer, morally grounded situation that will be life-giving or lifesaving for another? It doesn't have to be a situation of an addiction that puts us in this quandary. It can be a myriad of different situations such as the death of a child for a parent, the death of a loved one due to the coronavirus, the breakup of a stable relationship between lovers, the loss of a career or job due to the economy, or the illness of a family member or best friend with a very poor prognosis. All these challenges bring us to the brink of the fear of death or abandonment but at the same time trigger a spark of faith and hope, allowing us to escape the dread of the dire situation with a renewed future for a second chance to live again.

Here is where redemption for Scrooge lies. Not only is Scrooge using his new lease of life to make amends, but he is also forgiven by those characters who had been most personally affected by his cruelty. The transformation of Scrooge's life hinges on forgiveness, which is at the heart of Christian doctrine. Forgiveness is also at the heart of his redemption as it is for all of us. It is only through forgiveness that second chances are possible. Forgiveness is the self-giving gift that is redemption.

Unfortunately, both in the Victorian age and in our own, there is the erroneous belief of many that love means never having to say you're sorry.[53] When you are forgiven, which is one of the many facets of love, the saying "I am sorry" is not only implied but defines what love is about and what forgiveness entails. This mindset of not having to say "I am sorry" undermines the reality of forgiveness and is an affront to what love is. Forgiveness is a two-way street. It is bilateral between the offender and the one offended. Scrooge's redemption is totally conditioned upon not only owning his feelings of remorse for all his offenses toward others but also his need to seek out and make amends with those whom he injured through action. Scrooge does make amends not only with Bob Cratchit but also with his nephew Fred, also with one of the gentleman solicitors who collected for the poor whom he dismissed rudely, and with all the townspeople he had slighted all these years. Love and in turn forgiveness always mean and empower one to say, "I am sorry." Forgiveness becomes the dynamic that not only ensures peace between the offender and the injured party but also is necessary for one's redemption as a human being to maintain relationships and also be in good stead with the Almighty.

Scrooge's forgiving spirit and repentance are solidified in the final episode of the tale where he pretends to be beside himself over Cratchit's lateness in coming to work the day after Christmas. Scrooge's demeanor was very stern and deliberate as he called Cratchit into his office as Bob trembled, feeling that he was going to be fired as Scrooge began his remarks, "I am not going to stand for this sort of thing any longer…and therefore I am about to raise your salary… A merry Christmas, Bob!" said Scrooge with an earnestness that could not be mistaken as he clapped him on the back. "A merrier Christmas, Bob, my good fellow, than I have given you for many a year! I'll raise your salary, and endeavor to assist your struggling family, and we will discuss your affairs this very afternoon, over a Christmas bowl of smoking bishop,[54] Bob! Make up the fires and buy another coal-scuttle before you dot another I, Bob Cratchit!"

The tale's ending reminds us of the forgiveness and goodness exhibited by Tiny Tim and now is embraced by Scrooge. Scrooge's transformation not only redeems his own life but also saves Tiny Tim's life. Tiny Tim is saved through Scrooge's self-gift of renewed faith resulting in self-transformation. If Scrooge didn't reform with his last dream encounter with the Spirit of Christmas Yet to Come, he truly would have died at his grave site, and there would be no further mention of Tiny Tim. The story would have abruptly ended as a tragedy. Thanks to Scrooge's life decision to change from his evil ways to becoming a self-gift to others, his story continues through the years, and this tale becomes a cause for celebrating life and second chances. Since it relives the joy and spirit of celebrating family in festive traditions as recalled by all the good characters of the story despite their idiosyncrasies, it is a comedy of life. Time has turned tragedy into comedy. Time has changed the life of a wealthy miserable man into a man who valued human life due to his acceptance and belief in self-transformation. Time has allowed one to be given second chances.

It was this gratuitous reality of faith that awakened and sprung into Scrooge's life that he was able to reclaim his life. Without this faith, self-transformation would not be possible. Without self-transformation, redemption is not possible.

# CHAPTER 6

# Faithfulness as Ultimate Self-Transformation

---

But however, and whenever we part from one another, I am
sure we shall none of us forget poor Tiny Tim—shall we—
or this first parting that there was among us? And I know,
my dears, that when we recollect how patient and mild, he
was, although he was a little, little child, we shall not quarrel
easily among ourselves, and forget poor Tiny Tim in doing
it. Spirit of Tiny Tim, thy childish essence was from God!

—Bob Cratchit to his family

If you have ever watched a Western, you will have noticed that
most characters in the film fit into two categories: the pioneers
and the settlers. Pioneers are people who never like being tied
down in one place. They are always on the move. Their home is
usually the covered wagon, and they enjoy seeing new faces and new
frontiers. They are constantly vigilant in facing different settings in
different environments, protecting themselves from other travelers.

Then there are the settlers. They hate wandering and exploring
and put their roots in the land, build homes, and begin communities. They enjoy the routine of daily life and the security that comes

from being anchored in one place. They are vigilant about protecting their homesteads against wandering marauders.

In life, there are pioneers who experiment with different situations and settlers who are more conservative by being stayed and permanent figures. Self-transformation can occur with either type. Do you see yourself as a pioneer or a settler? Life is made up of both types. In fact, many times, one person can take either position depending upon their stage or situation in life. The virtue of faithfulness demands that one be both adventurous in taking risks for a loved one and yet at the same time be consistent and reliable as settlers are to always be present for the other.

These two roles easily apply to Tiny Tim, who is naturally adventurous as a child. Yet as a child, as he struggles with a chronic illness, he also exhibits the qualities of a settler by his steadfast love, devotion, and innocence toward his family. His reliability makes him the heartbeat of the Cratchit family. In fact, he is the soul of the entire tale, interestingly enough, without being the protagonist of the novella.

Faithfulness is Tiny Tim's other name. This crippled child whose appearances in the tale are dispersed throughout is always encouraging, always present, and always faithful to his family—the Cratchits. Ultimately, Tim's great virtue of faithfulness becomes the game changer for Scrooge, who not only develops a liking for Tim, but it was Tim's impending death as forecasted by the Spirit of Christmas Present that made Scrooge begin to reflect upon his own life, realizing life was too short. Scrooge begins to question his life of greed and avarice. This becomes a turning point in Scrooge's process of transformation and conversion.

"God bless us everyone!" said Tiny Tim, the last of all. He sat very close to his father's side, upon his little stool. Bob held his withered little hand in his, as if he loved the child, and wished to keep him by his side, and dreaded that he might be taken from him. "Spirit," said Scrooge *with an interest he had never felt before*, "tell me if Tiny Tim will live." "I see a vacant seat," replied the Ghost, "in the poor chimney-corner, and a crutch without an owner, carefully preserved.

If these shadows remain unaltered by the Future, the child will die." "No, no," said Scrooge. "Oh, no, kind Spirit, say he will be spared." "If these shadows remain unaltered by the Future, none other of my race," returned the Ghost, "will find him here. What then? If he be like to die, he had better do it, and decrease the surplus population." *Scrooge hung his head to hear his own words quoted by the Spirit and was overcome with penitence and grief* (stave 3—"The Second of the Three Spirits").

The Spirit of Christmas Present further reprimands Scrooge's hypocrisy: "Man," said the Ghost, "if man you be in heart, not adamant, forbear that wicked cant until you have discovered What the surplus is, and where it is. Will you decide what men shall live; what men shall die? It may be that, in the sight of Heaven, you are more worthless and less fit to live than millions like this poor man's child. Oh God! to hear the Insect on the leaf pronouncing on the too much life among his hungry brothers in the dust!" *Scrooge bent before the Ghost's rebuke and, trembling, cast his eyes upon the ground.* This was the turning point in Scrooge's process of reclaiming his life, the beginnings of self-transformation.

The tale takes an upswing and a more positive direction from here on. Scrooge begins to be critical of his past lifestyle, which, seemingly, a small child of nonimportance was responsible to redirect Scrooge to the light and away from the darkness. For without faithfulness, which is steadfastness and honest in any relationship as exemplified in Tiny Tim, self-transformation is not possible. For it is relationship built on faith that gives power, energy, and credibility for self-transformation. Faithfulness exhibits itself in behaviors of steadfast love, fidelity, reliability, understanding, compassion, and empathy.

Anything less is only an acquaintance and merely a semblance of a true friendship. Scrooge learned how to be a friend the hard way. After his love relationship with his lifetime sweetheart, Belle, his only semblance of friendship was his business association with his partner Jacob Marley. It is ironic that the faithfulness Scrooge began to embrace in dealing with humanity as the story unfolds came as a result of his partner's admonition that Scrooge needed to reform before it was too late. Timing is everything. Scrooge was able to reclaim his life before death, which was his redemption. However, his redemption had horizontal effects, for it became exemplary for others that it could happen despite what wrongs have been committed in the past.

Jacob Marley's admonition, which triggered Scrooge's conversion, did not do the same for Marley. He was not so fortunate. Time ran out.

One of Dickens's goal in writing his Christmas stories and also true of his "ghost stories" was to restore Christmas to its rightful place in London's society. *A Christmas Carol* would become one of the significant monuments of English literature in the Victorian age. Dickens's tale does not merely describe the season or its aspects as much as it embodies them in its character and actions.[55]

Celebrating the Christmas season despite puritan skepticism concerning the merriment of the feast had grown in popularity through the Victorian period with the introduction of the Christmas tree in Britain as popularized by Queen Victoria and Prince Albert. This along with the revival of interest in Christmas caroling influenced Dickens to write many tales about Christmas. His first story published in 1835 in the *Bell's Weekly Messenger* was entitled "A Christmas Dinner" in Sketches by Boz (1836). This was followed by "The Story of the Goblins Who Stole a Sexton," which appeared in the 1836 novel *The Pickwick Papers.*

Paul Davis, a Dickens literary expert, attests that the "Goblins" story appears to be a prototype of *A Christmas Carol.*

Although Dickens nominally was an Anglican, he was a vocal critic of organized religion, especially when he saw a hypocritical dichotomy between the preaching and the practice of Christian charity. Especially in many cases, he felt the Church of England, even with the benevolent reign of Queen Victoria, could have done more for the struggling poor in the major cities by promoting social justice to ensure socioeconomic equality of the populace and not leave it up to the power of lawmakers and politicians to figure it out. Dickens's attitudes toward organized religion were ambivalent, although he did profess his beliefs and principles on the New Testament of the Christian scriptures.[56]

Dickens did believe that Scrooge's conversion demonstrated that even the worst sinner can become righteous. This is further documented in Dickens characterizing that Marley "had no bowels" as a reference to the "bowels of compassion" as mentioned in the first letter of John in the New Testament.[57] Although as a young man he expressed a distaste for certain aspects of organized religion, he regarded himself as a professing Christian honoring the figure of Jesus Christ. His son Henry Fielding Dickens described his father as someone who "possessed deep religious convictions." He did author a work called *The Life of Our Lord* (1846), which was a book about the life of Christ written with the purpose of sharing faith with his children and family. Dickens had shown interest in Unitarian Christianity, although he never strayed from his attachment to Anglicanism.[58] He considered Roman Catholicism and nineteenth-century evangelicalism as both extremes of Christianity, which limited personal expression, and was critical of what he observed as the hypocrisy of religious institutions and philosophies like spiritualism, which he considered to be deviations from the true spirit of Christianity.

However, with his legitimate criticism of religion, many critics have suggested that in his little Christmas fable whether—consciously or unconsciously—he complemented the glorification of the nativity of Christ with a specific set of practices derived from Christ's example: charity and compassion in the form of educational opportunity, human conditions, and a decent life for all.[59]

I am not suggesting that Tiny Tim is a symbol of the Christ Child, but the chief focus of Scrooge's transformation is largely attributed to Tim as explained earlier. The portrayal of Tiny Tim—derived from Dicken's memories of his sickly younger brother, whom he called Tiny Fred—has proved "real" enough to prompt modern-day physicians to puzzle over the exact nature of the fictional child's affliction. Mostly likely, Tiny Tim and Tiny Fred suffered from rickets, a common affliction of that time in cities where smog frequently blocked sunlight, the natural source of vitamin D.[60] In many ways, Tiny Tim became the template of Scrooge's conversion to what faithfulness, friendship, and loyalty to family was about. Although there are no "holy" ghosts in *A Christmas Carol,* the three dream parables set a moral compass for Scrooge and most importantly for English society at the time.

Faithfulness as a road to human redemption was also exhibited by the graciousness and inspiring energy of Mrs. Cratchit, who never surrendered to the adversities of life. She was the glue that kept her large family of six children along with her husband as a happy, stable, and faith-filled family unit in dreadful economic times. Her authenticity, encouragement, strength, transparency, and faith were the soul of the Cratchits. As Tiny Tim was the heartbeat of the family, so too Mrs. Cratchit was the spiritual center of the Cratchits.

Redemption is defined to be the salvific consequences of one's actions. Analogous to faith in the Divine, no matter what the religious tradition is, it is redemptive for the believer to work out one's salvation in faith with the grace of God where eternal life becomes the prize, so too, with redemption in human terms through kindness, fidelity, compassion, righteousness, and justice, one finds serenity with self and harmony with the world. Redemption involves the paradox of finding oneself by losing oneself. The gospel of generosity, forgiveness, conversion, charity, hope, and faith, which *A Christmas Carol* evokes, is mirrored and complementary to the Christian gospel of service to others, love of neighbor, and belief in the power of the Christ Child.

The redemption of Scrooge as witnessed through his gradual transformation as processed through the dreams is not only central to the story but, as Paul Davis, a Dickens scholar, contends, Scrooge is a *protean figure* always in the process of reformation.

After all, isn't that what redemption is—a life process of seeking the truth, the light, and righteousness of one's existence over time? It is not magical and cannot be attained in one giant swoop but over a life span through different experiences, good, bad, and indifferent.

Richard Kelly, a Dickensian author, suggests that the transformation is reflected in the description of Scrooge, who begins as a two-dimensional character but who then grows as the tale develops into one who possesses an emotional depth and at the same time a regret for lost opportunities.[61] Another Dickens scholar, Grace Moore, suggests that a Christian theme runs through *A Christmas Carol*, and it should be seen as an allegory of the Christian concept of redemption.[62] In any event, Dickens's attempts to expose the character of Ebenezer Scrooge in the course of the story to paradigms of what faithfulness is so as to accept and embrace it lovingly. To that extent, it made Scrooge the ultimate transformative character.

# CHAPTER 7

# The End of It—The Gift of *A Christmas Carol*

God Bless Us. Everyone!

—Tiny Tim

Sometimes, when people point out something is wrong with us, we can see what they are saying, recognize it as true, but proceed to do nothing about it. I think that is one of the hurdles of human nature. We know from life experience that insight about oneself doesn't necessarily lead to change. Change is threatening in just thinking about doing something a different way than we are familiar in doing. Change makes us feel uneasy by focusing us in a different way about dealing with issues after having received some insight or by dialoguing with others who are different than us. We get so accustomed and comfortable with the dysfunctional ways of doing things in time that we postpone, procrastinate, or even deny that a new way is better. After all, what is the definition of insanity but to behave the same way over and over again, expecting a different outcome? This is not only dysfunctional but also unhealthy and perpetuates spinning our wheels in a frustrating and aimless way in life.

Unfortunately, discovering the truth about ourselves doesn't compel us to alter our ways, particularly when we are oversensitive when others suggest corrections in the way we do things or challenge our mindset about certain things. Our self-esteem is injured. The truth many times can stop us in our own tracks and have a paralyzing effect so as to motivate us to action. Many times, the prospect of change disheartens us and makes us fearful of doing something different. We get overwhelmed. We get frightened. We are set in our ways, and we are not ready, so we reject acting on positive and constructive criticism.

It touches upon our insecurity to change.

At the bottom of every constructive criticism lies the voice of encouragement, which motivates us that good can grow out of change or reform. Ironically, the emotional or spiritual paralysis one experiences when challenged by change fearing a loss of control of one's life becomes the very opportunity for one to take charge and assert one's control of their lives.

People begin to change when they are encouraged to see the best in themselves, not when they are asked to dwell with the worst in themselves. Simply to tell people what is wrong with them and leave it at that can leave them in a wreck. People rarely change when they are left with their own misery staring at their own mistakes and weaknesses. That is a dark and lonely place to dwell on past blunders and leaves little care whether change can take place or not. We all need help, support, and encouragement to leave behind the familiar dysfunctional ways, which have become arduous and sometimes destructive. We need help from others to imagine ourselves differently, imagining the good effect that we will have on others. We need to imagine ourselves as difference makers in others' lives, not intruders. We need faith in the future and hope in the present, working the change. In all this, we need to prod one another on by saying, "Go, you can do this!" We need to call out the best in people before we make demands about how others need to change. We need to be constantly breathing encouragement to others instead of judging better ways to do things. That will be a change for the better and may just compel people enough to act on the truth they have learned about themselves rather than tell others what to do. In the words of John Henry Newman, "To be human is to change, to be perfect is to have changed often."

It is appropriate for the last chapter or stave 5 to be entitled "The End of It," meaning at the end of what is said and done, the true gift of *A Christmas Carol* is a celebration of life. This is the moral of the tale and gift to us. Change and self-transformation only come at a price with faith and, with it, hope in self-redemption. Change is difficult but a life process accessible for all of us. The challenge in life is not to merely change for change's sake but to make alterations that are life-giving and difference makers for ourselves and others.

This we have seen with the character of Ebenezer Scrooge. The sin of Scrooge is not merely his disdain toward humanity of Christmases' past and unwillingness to change in Christmas' present because of greed and self-indulgence but his blindness of his own human potential to be a difference maker to bring joy, hope, and self-giving to others as he trotted toward Christmases' yet to come. The sin of Scrooge is that it took him almost half his lifetime to find and enjoy the friendship, compassion, forgiveness, and love of people, having been blinded by self-indulgence. Dickens recognized his own emotional and spiritual blindness as he came close to following in his father's footsteps of possibly ending up in beggars' prison. Dickens writes of his own self-transformation emerging from those lonely and dark evening walks through the London streets in composing the characters of Ebenezer Scrooge and the others in his novella. Ironically, the character of Scrooge, which Dickens created, became his muse for his own personal transformation both as a human being and as an author.

Another discovery made by Dickens for his own introspection, which was characterized in the life of Scrooge and which we can relate to in our own life journeys, is that feelings cause pain. Although our feelings are good, important, and we all need to be in touch with them, it is feelings that bring passion to life. It is feelings that "stirs the pot" and initiates change. Along with our intellect and soul, it is feelings that make us human. Scrooge was incapable to reach into those feelings after his separation for his first love, Belle, and for whatever reason he needed to find a replacement to believe that he has worth. So he turned to becoming successful by becoming wealthy to fill that gap. How do we acknowledge and channel our feelings?

It is real to acknowledge that many times feelings bring pain, resulting from the death of a loved one, the ending of a love affair, the betrayal of a friend, the loss of one's career or job, or the loss of health due to illness. All these are real but do not need to paint the picture of any entire life. Feelings can also bring ecstasy when one is loved, self-worth when one has the opportunity to love, competence when one discovers and becomes good at what they do in life, and consolation and reconciliation when one is forgiving or receives forgiveness. All these positive feelings Scrooge lost out on until the presence of a little child brought these feelings to the surface for him. In turn, these feelings ignited a new way of thinking about oneself and the world. In turn, many times, it is feelings that causes us to restructure thoughts, resulting in self-transformation.

The conversion of Scrooge from self-indulgence, narcissism, abuse of power, and hypocrisy to angelic love brought him peace and harmony with the world. All of us have our own London dark streets to walk reflecting upon our own particular blindness in living even though it may not lead us to beggars' prison. However, nonetheless, it is a road less travelled for the fainthearted and those who fear life's challenges. However, for those who seek these new roads to find the courage to be *as* Oneself by finding themselves and restoring their own dignity and respect toward others, it is more than a Christmas carol but human redemption. A valued lesson we can all learn from this Christmas tale is the importance of being grateful for who we are and what we have.

This Irish saying is appropriate here at this time, "I shall pass this way but once, if there is any good word or deed, I can render let me do it now for I shall not pass this way again." Only this altruistic mindset *can bring about the fruits expressed in another Irish blessing—"May you live as long as you want and not want as long as you live."*

*A Christmas Carol* teaches us all that we are blessed and loved each day not because we regret for lacking the things we feel we should have but because we cherish the things and people in our lives whom we do have. We cherish our faith, family, friends, health, and a future to live forever. These are what makes us human.

This is what makes humanity divine!

Dickens's father is said to have led the family in the following prayer at the Christmas dinner celebration: "'Let this day be the fragrance of the love we bear for one another. God bless us, everyone!"

Interestingly enough, Dickens incorporated this prayer in Tiny Tim's invitation to enjoy, cherish, and share with others the blessings of Christmas but most importantly the blessings of the rest of our lives.

Our faith and hopes for the people we care for can be summarized in Tiny Tim's prayer, "God bless us everyone!"

Andrea Bocelli captured this sentiment in these lyrics of his famous classic Christmas carol (I would suggest you look up this tune on YouTube to listen for its musical accompaniment, which is very inspiring).

Come together, one and all
In the giving spirit
Gifts abound here great and small
Joyously we feel it
Blessings sent us from above
Guide us on our way
We raise our voice as we rejoice
Bow our head and pray
A miracle has just begun
**God bless us everyone**
To the voices no one hears
We have come to find you

With your laughter and your tears
Goodness, hope and virtue
Father, Mother, Daughter, Son
Each a treasure be
One candle's light dispels the night
Now our eyes can see
Buried brighter than the sun
**God bless us everyone**
The miracle has just begun
**God bless us everyone**
Come together one and all
In the giving spirit
Gifts abound here great and small
Joyously we feel it
Father, Mother, Daughter, Son
Each a treasure be
One candle's light dispels the night
Now our eyes can see
Burning brighter than the sun
**God bless us everyone**
The miracle has just begun
**God bless us everyone**
(Source: Musixmatch)

Songwriters: Alan Menken/Lynne Ahrens
God Bless Us Everyone lyrics @Walt Disney Music Company,
Trunksong Music Ltd 2018

Scrooge was better than his word. He did it all, and infinitely more, and to Tiny Tim, who did NOT die, he was a second father. He became as good a friend, as good a master, and as good a man as the good old city knew or any other good old city, town, or borough in the good old world. Some people laughed to see the alteration in him, but he let them laugh and little heeded them, for he was wise enough to know that nothing ever happened on this globe, for good, at which some people did not have their fill of laughter in the outset; and knowing that such as these would be blind anyway, he thought it quite as well that they should wrinkle up their eyes in grins as have the malady in less attractive forms. His own heart laughed, and that was quite enough for him.

He had no further intercourse with spirits but lived upon the total abstinence principle ever afterward, and it was always said of him that he knew how to keep Christmas well, if any man alive possessed the knowledge. May that be truly said of us, and all of us! And so as Tiny Tim observed, God bless us, every one! (stave 5—"The End of It").

# Summary of *A Christmas Carol*

*Stave 1*

The tale begins on a bleak, cold Christmas Eve in London, seven years after the death of Ebenezer Scrooge's business partner, Jacob Marley. Scrooge is an aging miser, dislikes Christmas, and refuses a dinner invitation from his nephew Fred, the son of Fan, Scrooge's dead sister. As proprietor of a counting house, he keeps a cruel monopoly on the coal supply in his office and keeps his overworked and underpaid clerk, Bob Cratchit, shivering in the cold. Subsequently, Scrooge turns away two gentlemen who seek a donation from him to feed, clothe, and house the poor. He believes in keeping the poor in workhouses, claiming he has supported the establishments designed to keep prisons and treadmills in operation. Scrooge grudgingly allows his clerk, Bob Cratchit, Christmas Day off with pay to conform to social custom.

After Scrooge took his melancholy dinner in his usual melancholy tavern that evening, he arrives at his home once owned by Jacob Marley. He is greeted by a series of spooky apparitions. First, his door knocker turns into Marley's face. It was seven years prior on Christmas Eve that Marley died. Scrooge refuses to believe his senses and hurries upstairs. That night, he is visited at home by the full-length spirit of Marley, bound in a huge, clanking chains and money boxes forged during a lifetime of greed and selfishness. Marley tells Scrooge that he has been wandering the earth, aimlessly trying to undo the wrongs that he neglected in his lifetime. Marley warns Scrooge that he is destined for the same fate and even worse. He tells Scrooge that he has a single chance to avoid this same fate: he will be visited by three spirits and must listen or be cursed to carry much heavier chains of his own. Marley's ghost disappears, and Scrooge falls into a deep sleep.

*Stave 2*

When Scrooge awakens, it is still dark, as if no time passed. He is cynical and questions what he has just experienced. He is greeted by the first spirit, the Ghost of Christmas Past, appearing as a candle-like apparition that is brightly glowing, shedding light to the whole room. This spirit takes Scrooge to Christmas scenes of Scrooge's childhood, reminding him of the time when he was more innocent. The scene reveals Scrooge's lonely childhood at boarding school, recalling his relationship with his beloved sister Fan. His sister Fan comes to bring him home. Subsequently, Scrooge sees himself as an apprentice at a Christmas party hosted by his first employer, Mr. Fezziwig—it was a joyous time of food, dance, and music. For Fezziwig treated him as a son. Then Scrooge is tortured by the memory that his neglected fiancée, Belle, is shown ending their relationship, breaking off their engagement as she realizes that he will never love her as much as he loves money. Finally, Scrooge and the spirit visit a now married Belle with her large, happy family on the Christmas Eve that Marley died. Scrooge is left upset by hearing Belle's description of the man that he has become, demands that the spirit remove him from the house. The spirit is extinguished, and as darkness enveloped the room, Scrooge falls asleep.

*Stave 3*

As Scrooge awakens, he is greeted by the loud bellowing voice of the Ghost of Christmas Present. The spirit's presence fills his apartment with warmth and intense light. The apparition was that of a gentle giant in a fur festive robe sitting atop a feast of Christmas food. This ghost takes Scrooge to a joyous market with people buying the makings of Christmas dinner. As they fly through the streets invisibly, visiting the merry townspeople and the spirit sprinkling the magic incense on their dinners to make them filled with joy, they come to Bob Cratchit's family house. Scrooge witnesses the joy of how the Cratchits prepare for the great feast. Scrooge also notices that Bob brings his crippled son, Tiny Tim, home upon his shoulders and tells his wife that their son is doing better. Tim's bravery and gentleness of voice fill the house, and this touches Scrooge to the extent that he inquires of the spirit if the boy will live. But the spirit cannot promise Scrooge that Tiny Tim will survive his illness unless the course of events changes. Afterward, the spirit and Scrooge travel to celebrations of Christmas in a miner's cottage in a lighthouse and on a ship at sea. Scrooge and the ghost then visit his nephew Fred's Christmas party. There Scrooge witnesses a gala celebration of Christmas with friends singing songs, playing games, and enjoying one another's company, often ridiculing Uncle Scrooge. Scrooge is taken up with invisibly playing along with the games, but it ends abruptly when the spirit's time is up. The spirit leaves Scrooge with the vision of two impoverished, hideous, emaciated children sheltered under the spirit's robe, named Ignorance and Want, and tells Scrooge to beware them and mocks Scrooge's concern for their welfare.

*Stave 4*

The third and final spirit comes toward Scrooge enrobed in a black cloak so that all Scrooge can see is his eerily pointing bony hand. This Ghost of Christmas Yet to Come was the one Scrooge feared the most. Although terrified, Scrooge was eager to see where this spirit would lead him. Scrooge is led to the trading district where businessmen are casually discussing the death of a disliked man whose funeral is attended by the local businessmen only on condition that lunch is provided. No one seemed upset about this man's death but rather amused and happy about it. Then the spirit brings Scrooge to witness a group of scavengers, trading in the dead man's possessions for money. Scrooge is transported to a dark room where he sees the corpse itself covered with a cloth. He begs the spirit to see some tender emotions or tears shed for this man's death, but all the ghost can show him is a family who are relived at his death because it lifts their debt, and the house of Bob Cratchit, which is overcome with grief at the loss of Tiny Tim. Scrooge implores the ghost to show him his own fate, and the spirit directs him to a neglected grave in a churchyard with a tombstone bearing Scrooge's name. He is beside himself with fear and sadness and desperately promises the spirit that he will keep Christmas in his heart from now on. The spirit vanishes, and he awakens in tears.

*Stave 5*

Scrooge awakens overwhelmed with joy, and he realizes he is not doomed like his partner Jacob Marley but that he has the opportunity to change his future. He cannot contain his joy as he laughs and shakes uncontrollably upon discovering that it is Christmas morning and survived the great ordeal of the ghost visitations. He makes a large donation to the charity he rejected the previous day and anonymously sends a large prize turkey to the Cratchits' home for Christmas dinner. He cannot contain his joy greeting everyone he meets on the street with a merry Christmas and goes to his nephew's house to celebrate Christmas with Fred's family. The next day, he gives Cratchit a raise for his work and over the ensuing years helps ensure that Tiny Tim not only survives but also thrives and becomes a father figure to Tiny Tim. From then on, Scrooge treats everyone with kindness, generosity, respect, and compassion, embodying the spirit of Christmas.

# Major Characters

---

*Ebenezer Scrooge*—The quintessential miser, cruelhearted proprietor of a counting house who significantly underpays his clerk, Bob Cratchit, who receives fifteen shillings for a six-day work-week. In Victorian currency, 1 shilling was worth about 12 pennies. Scrooge took over Marley's part of the business upon his death since they had been business partners, and he also helped himself to all of Marley's assets, house, and possessions. His famous response to a Christmas greeting was "humbug," which colloquially meant a hoax, sham, imposition, or used interjectionally to mean "stuff and nonsense," When he is visited by his deceased partner's ghost, Jacob Marley, he begins to consider the error of his ways, and through a series of dreams, he is shown his own past; the sight of his neglected childhood Christmases begins to explain why he began his downward spiral into misery. He reflects upon the current celebrations of Christmas in the present and is frightened and regretful when he sees the vivid images of Christmas yet to come, which predictably leaves him dying alone. Scrooge reverses his way of life from being greedy and absorbed by wealth to being altruistic and an advocate of Christmas cheer.

*Ghost of Christmas Past*—A strange combination of young and old, this spirit has the innocence of an infant but is seen as if through a veil of time, as if he is very elderly. This ghost is described as having white robes and glows as a flame of light. At the end of his tour with Scrooge, this light is extinguished with a cap, making it clear that it is reborn and dies again every Christmas. This spirit directs Scrooge to scenes of past Christmases.

*The Ghost of Christmas Yet to Come*—This is the most ominous of all the spirits, described as robed in black, silent, and leads the way with an eerily pointed bony finger toward the disturbing visions of Scrooge's future, eventually leading him to his own lonely gravestone. This spirit culminates the moral lesson of the story.

*Bob Cratchit*—Scrooge's loyal clerk who is very poorly treated by his boss, Ebenezer Scrooge. He is the devoted husband and father of six children whose large family live in cold and poverty. The eldest children work hard, and Bob is always looking to find them better situations. His youngest, Tiny Tim, is a cripple and the light of his life but is very ill and needs medical attention that Bob cannot afford. Bob is the optimum example of the virtues of Christmas and provides the antidote to Scrooge's greed. Bob is also a symbol of human empathy and forgiveness, for he toasts Scrooge at the family Christmas dinner despite his horrendous work conditions. As opposed to Scrooge's remorseful ending, Bob is congenial and accepting of life rather than being bitter and resentful.

*Tiny Tim*—This is Bob Cratchit's crippled son and can be seen usually sitting on his father's shoulder or struggling along with his crutch. Besides being the bearer of human suffering, he is portrayed as the merriest, bravest of all the characters and is a constant reminder of the goodness and generosity shared at Christmas. It is the fixed thought of Tiny Tim's inevitable death due to his illness as confirmed in the vision of the Ghost of the Christmas Yet to Come that fills Scrooge with regret and ultimately becomes the motivation for Scrooge to change his life. Tiny Tim's prayer becomes the eminent theme of Dickens's Christmas tale—"God bless us everyone!"

*Jacob Marley*—He was Scrooge's former business partner. He was nevertheless Scrooge's only friend despite Scrooge not being particularly sorrowful upon his death. He becomes the figure that haunts and protects Scrooge by appearing early in the tale as the door knocker of Scrooge's home and introduces the three Christmas spirits. He makes manifest the horror of regret with the burdensome chain and describes how he is doomed to wander the earth aimlessly for eternity, a fate that Scrooge will face unless he changes his ways.

*Minor Characters*

*Fan*—She is Scrooge's younger sister and Fred's mother. Scrooge loved her dearly, but she died young with childbirth. She is deceased at the time of the story, but in the first vision of the Ghost of Christmas Past, she comes to visit Scrooge in a deserted schoolroom when he was a child, and she convinces their father to allow Ebenezer to return home from school one Christmas. She is the symbol of loving-kindness and has always been loyal and faithful to her brother.

*Fred*—He is Scrooge's kindhearted nephew who loves Christmas and pities his miserly uncle because although he is wealthy, he is alone and miserable. Each year, he invites Scrooge to Christmas dinner, only to be refused and ridiculed by Scrooge, who remarks, "Bah humbug." He refuses to let Scrooge's negative attitude dampen his Christmas cheer and insists that he will visit his uncle each year on Christmas Eve and invite him regardless of Scrooge's refusal to accept Christmas greetings.

*Mr. Fezziwig*—He is a jovial, selfless merchant to whom Scrooge is apprenticed as a young man. He along with his family are very generous to their employees and to all the townspeople and are renowned for his wonderful Christmas parties celebrated each year. His generosity makes Scrooge feel guilty on how poorly he treats his own sole employee, Bob Cratchit.

*Mrs. Cratchit*—She is Bob's kind and loving wife, who holds little patience and love for Scrooge. She is Bob's great support and life companion who is the loving mother of their six children. In many adaptations of the tale, she was referred to as Emily.

*Belle*—She is Scrooge's young love who breaks off their engagement because of his misplaced priorities of greed and his preoccupation of material things over their love. When they met, Scrooge was happy to be poor with her, but money became his idol.

*The Ghost of Christmas Present*—This was the second spirit to visit and tour with Scrooge. He is described as a loud, portly, jovial, giant clad in green robe spreading Christmas cheer with his life span restricted to one day. He is surrounded by a warm glow and feast-like piles of food carrying a cornucopia, a sort of horn with special powers to bestow seasonal joy on the neediest townsfolk.

*The Cratchit children*—The Cratchits have six children—the oldest son, Peter; their oldest daughter, Martha, who works in the milliner's shop; Tiny Tim; along with another daughter Belinda and two smaller children, a boy and a girl unnamed.

*The two soliciting gentlemen*—These two charitable workers visit Scrooge at the outset of the story, seeking contributions for the poor and destitute. Scrooge turns them down and throws them out of his office while insisting that he already supports government institutions that are designed to provide aid for the workhouses and prisons. After his transformation, Scrooge meets one of them on the street and offers a large sum of money for their charitable cause.

*The debtors*—They are the people or in this case a young couple who owed Scrooge an amount of money that they cannot repay. Upon learning of Scrooge's death, they are relieved in hopes that the new creditor who will assume the debt will be more lenient.

*Old Joe, Mrs. Dilber, Laundress, and the Undertaker*—This group of thieves meet at Old Joe's pawnshop to sell Scrooge's belongings that they stole from him after his death. They harbor no remorse or guilt for their thievery based on the fact that Scrooge was a cruel, miserly old man, and there was no one else to whom he could leave his wealth. In fact, Mrs. Dilber had served as Scrooge's housekeeper while he was alive.

# Other Stories for Christmas by Charles Dickens

---

- *The Chimes: A Goblin Story*
- *The Cricket on the Hearth: A Fairy Tale of Home* (1845)
- *A Christmas Tree* (1850)
- *What Christmas Is as We Grow Older* (1851)
- *The Poor Relation's Story* (1852)
- *The Child's Story* (1852)
- *The Schoolboy's Story* (1853)
- *Nobody's Story* (1854)
- *The Seven Poor Travelers* (1854)
- *The Holly-Tree* (1855)
- *The Wreck of the Golden Mary* (1856)
- *The Perils of Certain English Prisoners*
- Going into Society (1858)

*Christmas Stories from All the Year Round*

"The Haunted House" (1859)
"A Message from the Sea"
"Tom Tiddler's Ground" (1861)
*Somebody's Luggage* (1862)

# NOTES

---

1  Paulette Beete, "Ten Things to Know about Charles Dickens' *A Christmas Carol*." http://www.arts.gov/stories/blog/2020.

2  Frank Marzials, *Life of Charles Dickens*, including a Biography of Dickens by Sir Leslie Stephen: A Restored Special Edition (Philadelphia: CGR Publishing, 2021), p. 170–171.

3  Ibid., p. 169.

4  Ibid., p. 170.

5  Les Standiford, *The Man Who Invented Christmas* (New York: Broadway Books, 2017), p. 103–104.

6  Ibid., p. 196–197.

7  Ibid., p. 208–209.

8  John Forster, *The Life of Charles Dickens* (Published in Philadelphia: 1872–1874).

9  Les Standiford. op. cit., p. 62.

10  Ibid., p. 65.

11  Ibid., p.77–78.

12  Samantha Silva, *Mr. Dickens and His Carol* (New York: Flatirons Books, 2017) p.107f. Eleanor Lovejoy is a fictitious character introduced in Silva's novel as a personification of Dickens's inner conflicts, which he needed to confront and resolve leading to his composition of *A Christmas Carol.*

13  Ibid., p. 127f.

14  Ibid., p. 128.

15  Jonathan H. Grossman, *Charles Dickens's Networks: Public Transport and the Novel* (Oxford University Press, 2012). Cf. also David Lodge, *Consciousness and the Novel* (Harvard University Press, 2002), p.118.

16  Rich Bowen, *A Christmas Carol: Glossary, Commentary and Notes* (2004).

17  E. W. F. Tomlin, ed. *Charles Dickens 1812-1870, A Centennial Volume* (New York: Simon and Schuster,1969), p.45.

18  Ibid.

19  Charles Dickens *The Selected Letters of Charles Dickens* (London: Oxford University Press, 2012) p.171.

20  E. W. F. Tomlin, op. cit., p.93.

21 "Love Is a Many Splendored Thing." According to *Wikipedia*, lyrics were written by Paul Francis Webster and music composed by Sammy Fain released on March 26, 1962. The song was publicized first in the movie *Love Is a Many Splendored Thing* (1955), winning the Academy Award for best original song.

22 The Bible, RSV edition (San Francisco: Ignatius Press, 2006).

23 Albert Einstein (1879–1955) was a German-born theoretical physicist who developed the theory of relativity, one of two pillars of modern physics, the other being Max Karl Planck (1858–1947), father of energy quantum physics.

24 Paul Tillich *Dynamics of Faith* (New York: Harper One Publishers, 1957), p. 1–4.

25 Paul Tillich was a prolific German author, scholar, and Lutheran pastor who escaped the Nazi regime and migrated in the US where he became a dynamic teacher, charismatic preacher, Protestant theologian, and existential philosopher. He taught in a number of universities in Germany before migrating to the US in 1933 where he taught theology at Union Theological Seminary, Harvard Divinity School, and at the University of Chicago.

26 *Dynamics of Faith*, op. cit., p. 4 f.

27 Rich Bowen, op. cit., *A Christmas Carol: Glossary, Commentary and Notes* (2004). https://drbacchus.com/files/christmascarolglossary.pdf.

28 Lauren Boivin, instructor of lecture: Mrs. Cratchit in *A Christmas Carol* (March 19, 2018). https://study.com/academy/lesson/mrs-cratchit-in-a-christmas-carol.html.

29 Catherine Upchurch *Daily Reflections for Advent and Christmas: Waiting in Joyful Hope 2021-2022* (Collegeville, Minnesota: Liturgical Press, 2021).

30 Madeleine Delbrêl (1904–1964) was a French Catholic author, poet, and mystic whose works include *The Marxist City as Mission Territory* (1957), *The Contemporary Forms of Atheism* (1962), and the posthumous publications *We, the Ordinary People of the Streets* (1966) and *The Joy of Believing* (1968). She evangelized Christianity in France especially among the youth after her conversion from atheism. She devoted herself to the care of the poor and to the social needs of women in France.

31 Dorothy Day (1897–1980) was an American journalist, social activist, and considered by many to be an anarchist due to her progressive views of civil disobedience, economic theory of distributism, endorsing pacifism, and combining direct aid for the poor and homeless with nonviolent direct action on their behalf, which resulted in public demonstrations and arrests. She cofounded the *Catholic Worker* newspaper in 1933, which advocated for the disadvantaged and marginalized.

32 Madeleine Delbrêl, quotation taken from a selection of her works as it appeared in *Magnificat* (February 2022 edition, vol. 23, no. 12).

33 Carl G. Jung (1875–1961), Swiss psychiatrist and psychanalyst, founded analytical psychology. He is noted for his concept of individuation—lifelong psychological process of differentiation of the self.

34 Wallace B. Clift *Jung and Christianity: The Challenge of Reconciliation* (New York: Crossroads, 2000), p.105.

35 Ibid. p. 104.

36 Carl Jung, *Memories, Dream, Reflections* (1961). Jung directed that this autobiography not be included in his collected works of his writings and not be published until after his death, fearing possible criticism it would receive since his work was too personal and too uncommon at the time.

37 Jung, *Collected Works* XII, ed. Sir Herbert Read, et al. trans. R. F. C. Hull (2nd edition rev.; Bollinger Series) (Princeton, New Jersey: Princeton University Press, 1970), p.87.

38 Carl Jung formulated twelve universal mythic characters residing within our unconsciousness. They include the ruler, the creator/artist, the sage, the innocent, the explorer, the rebel, the hero, the wizard, the jester, "every man or every woman," the lover, and the caregiver. These symbolic images unconsciously understood and defined the range of basic human motivations. Jung in extrapolating his theory of the psyche identified four major archetypes—*the self* (sense of unity in experience with the goal of self-actualization); *the persona* or mask, which is the outward face we present as the desirable self to the world seeking acceptance from others; the *shadow*, the animal side of personality that is irrational, instinctive, and impulsive; *and the anima/animus*, the true self and primary source of communication with collective unconscious.

39 Jung, op. cit., *Collected Works.* XI

40 Athanasius of Alexandria (c. 296–373 CE) was bishop in Alexandria, Egypt, for forty-six years, renowned theologian of the Eastern Church of the patristic period (late first century to end of eighth century CE) who was a staunch defender of the Christian doctrine of the Incarnation of Jesus Christ and the Trinity. The quotation that "God became man so that man might become God" is attributed to him in defining the doctrine that Jesus Christ is a divine person of the Trinity at the same time having two natures: divine and human as eventually promulgated by the Council of Nicaea (325 CE).

41 John Henry Newman (1801–1890) was an English theologian, scholar, and poet, first an Anglican priest and converted to Catholicism, later becoming a Catholic priest and cardinal. He was an important and controversial figure in the religious history of England in the nineteenth century.

42 Paul Tillich was a German Lutheran theologian and existential philosopher of the twentieth century who fled the Nazi regime in the 1930s and migrated in the US, becoming a professor and lecturer at Yale University in Connecticut. His work *The Courage to Be* (1952) was his response to modern man's alienation of self caused by anxiety. The courage to be is the ethical act in which the human being affirms one's own being in spite of those elements of his existence that conflicts with one's meaning in life.

43 Rollo May *Love and Will,* (New York: Dell Publishing, 1969) p.123.

44 Ibid.

45 Rollo May, PhD (1909–1994), was an American existential psychologist and author of the influential book *Love and Will* (1969).

He is often associated with humanistic psychology and existential philosophy mostly noted for his theory that human beings fear death because we cannot comprehend our own lack of existence. He believed facing these feelings of anxiety and fear was a necessary experience if personal growth and meaning were to be achieved in life.

46 *Love and Will*, op. cit., p. 151.

47 Rich Bowen, op. cit., *A Christmas Carol: Glossary, Commentary and Notes* (Christmas 2004, https://drbacchus.com/files/christmas-carolglossary.pdf), Scrooge suggests that the poor go to the union workhouses or to the treadmill or that they be taken care of by the Poor Law. These things can be thought of as the welfare system of the time, although that's somewhat an oversimplification. The union workhouses were workhouses run by the local parish. When you were sent to the workhouse, this was referred to as "going on the parish." People were sent there if they were poor or in debt or otherwise destitute. There they would work to perform menial labor in exchange for their daily food and lodging. Exactly what they did in these workhouses varied from one place to another, but it was always backbreaking menial work. People who had gone on the parish were considered to be the lowest, and even poor people held them in contempt, knowing that they, too, were a week's wages away from going to the workhouse themselves. A child that grew up in the workhouse would often get the disparaging nickname of "Work us" or "Parish."

48 Jon Sindell, *A Christmas Carol: Annotated for Dickens Enthusiasts and Students Alike* (San Francisco: Smush Publications, 2020), p. 11.

49 Ibid.

50 Joshua E. Brinkman et al., *Physiology of Sleep* (Treasure Island, Florida: Stats Pearls Publishing, 2022).

51 Eric Suni, *Dreams,* article as found in sleepfoundation.org, updated March 18, 2022.

52 Imogen Lee, *Ragged Schools.* British Library. Retrieved January 8, 2017.

53 The expression "Love means never having to say you're sorry" comes from the movie *Love Story* starring Ali MacGraw and Ryan O'Neal.

54 Rich Bowen, op. cit., smoking bishop referred to a mulled wine, made with deep red wine, the color of a bishop's robes.

55 Les Standiford, op. cit., p. 178–179.

56 Martin H. Sable, "The Day of Atonement in Charles Dickens' *A Christmas Carol*" in *Tradition: A Journal of Orthodox Jewish Thought* 22, 3 (autumn 1986): pp. 66–76.

57 Robert Douglas-Fairhurst, "Introduction" in Charles Dickens (ed.) *A Christmas Carol and Other Christmas Books* (Oxford: Oxford Press, 2006), pp. vii–xxix.

58  Gary Colledge, *God and Charles Dickens: Recovering the Christian Voice of a Classic Author* (Brazos Press, 2012), p. 24.
59  Les Standiford, op. cit., p. 180.
60  Ibid., p. 181.
61  Richard Michael Kelly, "Introduction" in Charles Dickens (ed.) *A Christmas Carol* (Ontario: Broadway Press, 2003), p. 9–30.
62  Grace Moore, *Charles Dickens' A Christmas Carol* (St. Kilda VIC: Insight Publications, 2011).

# ABOUT THE AUTHOR

Louis Marini, MS, MSW, MDiv, JCL—through his multidisciplinary expertise and experience in pastoral ministry as a former Catholic priest of seventeen years, an ecclesiastical jurist, a researcher, an educator, and a clinician in the areas of psychology, social work, theology, and canon law—shares his reflections concerning the relevance of faith and its influence on self-transformation in our time. After practicing as a counseling psychologist and psychotherapist for over twenty-four years, he hopes to offer solace to former patients, students, and parishioners to whom he served in the past along with you, the reader. He received his graduate degrees from Catholic University of America, Washington, DC; Fordham University, New York City; Iona College, New Rochelle, New York; and Saint Joseph Seminary, Yonkers, New York. He completed postgraduate work at the Minuchin Center for the Family (1999) and studies in chemical dependency at Maxwell Institute in Tuckahoe, New York (2000–2001). He was a member of the American Psychological Association and the National Association of Social Workers until 2020 upon retirement from practice.